Storytime From A to Z

Activities That Build Early Literacy Skills Through the Sharing of Popular Children's Books

- Phonemic Awareness
- Letter Recognition
- Letter-Sound Relationships
- Listening Comprehension
- Reading Comprehension
- Writing

And More Important Skills!

Managing Editor: Allison E. Ward

Editorial Team: Becky S. Andrews, Kimberley Bruck, Karen P. Shelton, Diane Badden, Thad H. McLaurin, Sharon Murphy, Kimberly Brugger-Murphy, Cindy K. Daoust, Karen A. Brudnak, Sarah Hamblet, Hope Rodgers, Dorothy C. McKinney, Randi Austin, Eva Bareis, Jill Davis, Roxanne LaBell Dearman, Danna DeMars, Margaret Elliot, Angie Kutzer, Alison LaManna, Lisa Leonardi, Heather Miller, Jana Sanderson, Katie Zuehlke

Production Team: Lisa K. Pitts, Pam Crane, Clevell Harris, Rebecca Saunders, Jennifer Tipton Cappoen, Chris Curry, Sarah Foreman, Theresa Lewis Goode, Ivy L. Koonce, Clint Moore, Greg D. Rieves, Barry Slate, Donna K. Teal, Tazmen Carlisle, Amy Kirtley-Hill, Kristy Parton, Debbie Shoffner, Cathy Edwards Simrell, Lynette Dickerson, Mark Rainey

www.themailbox.com

Table of Contents

How to Use This Book

Each *Storytime From A to Z* unit features a popular children's book as well as four to six literacy-rich activities centered around a particular letter of the alphabet and the theme of the book. Use all the activities in the unit or just select the ones that best meet the needs of your students. To help you quickly and easily navigate each unit, icons have been added to the left of each activity title.

Prereading Activity

During or After Reading Activity

Letter-Based Activity
Letter will change with each unit.

Theme-Based Activity
Icon will reflect the theme of the featured book.

Craft Activity*

Music Activity*

*Included in some units.

Book Notes
To help students continue the learning at home, check out page 108, where you'll find information on how to use the reproducible book notes (letters home) provided for the featured books.

We read **A House for Hermit Crab** by Eric Carle.

Help me look around our house for things that start with *H*.

©The Mailbox® • *Storytime From A to Z* • TEC60878

©2005 The Mailbox®
All rights reserved.
ISBN #1-56234-639-3

Manufactured in the United States
10 9 8 7 6 5 4 3 2

A Is for Alligator!

There's an Alligator Under My Bed

Written and Illustrated by Mercer Mayer

A little boy knows there is an alligator under his bed, but his parents can't see it! So he decides to take matters into his own hands. Youngsters are sure to rest easier after watching this little boy triumph over the alligator, which is lured out from under the bed with a tempting trail of treats!

THERE'S AN ALLIGATOR UNDER MY BED

written and illustrated by MERCER MAYER

Who's Afraid?

Using prior knowledge

Is everyone afraid of scaly, toothy, four-legged reptiles? Nope! But everyone is afraid of something! Have youngsters discuss common fears with this simple prereading activity. Encourage students to name some common fears, such as snakes, monsters, spiders, and the dark. Then ask them whether alligators might be considered scary. After youngsters share their thoughts about alligators, explain that the story you're about to read is about a little boy who finds a way to get rid of an alligator. Then have youngsters get ready for an entertaining read-aloud.

Hiding Places

Developing a story innovation

The alligator in the story chooses to hide under a bed. But an imaginary alligator might show up anywhere! Have youngsters brainstorm other locations for the alligator with this class book. To begin, ask students where an imaginary alligator might be found, such as in a closet, under a sink, or in a garage. Then give each child a sheet of 12" x 18" white construction paper labeled with the prompt shown. Have each youngster complete the prompt and draw a picture to match. Then bind the pages together with a cover titled "Where Is the Alligator?" Read the completed book to your youngsters before placing it in your independent reading center. Little ones are sure to snap up this reading choice!

Where Is the Alligator? by Ms. Clark's class

There's an alligator undr the dresr.

A-a-alligator Armor
Recognizing the short A sound

Youngsters supply this alligator with its distinctive bony plates and practice the short A sound at the same time! Cut from green bulletin board paper a large alligator shape and tape it to a tabletop. Make a green construction paper copy of the picture cards on page 6. Cut the cards apart and then place them near the alligator cutout. A small group of children visits the table, and each child, in turn, chooses a card. She says the name of the picture and identifies whether it contains the short A sound. If it does, she places the card on the alligator's back. If it doesn't, she places the card in a separate pile. The children continue until all the cards have been chosen. For more practice with the short A sound, have each child complete a copy of page 7.

Later, Alligator!
Completing a writing prompt

How would your youngsters get rid of alligators under their beds? You'll find out when students practice writing skills with this crafty alligator! Gather the supplies below and then guide each youngster through the directions shown to make an alligator. When the alligator is dry, write the prompt shown on its snout. Help each student write a sentence on the alligator's tongue to complete the prompt. Go away, alligator!

Supplies:

hole puncher
2 green construction paper heads
length of white yarn
scissors
stapler
pink construction paper tongue

glue
two 3 oz. paper cups
green tempera paint
paintbrush
2 white construction paper eyes
black marker

Setup:

Hole-punch the edge of one alligator head as shown. To keep the yarn from being pulled through while lacing, tie an end of the length of yarn to the first hole.

Steps:

1. Lace the yarn through the holes in the head cutout. (Tie the remaining end to the last hole and clip off any extra yarn.)
2. Glue the tongue to the remaining head cutout. (Staple the cutouts together to make an upper and a lower jaw.)
3. Paint the cups green. Allow the paint to dry.
4. Use the marker to draw pupils on the eyes. Then glue an eye to each cup.
5. Glue the cups to the head. Set the project aside to dry.

If there were an alligator under my bed... I would jump up and down on my bed until he came out.

Picture Cards
Use with "A-a-alligator Armor" on page 5.

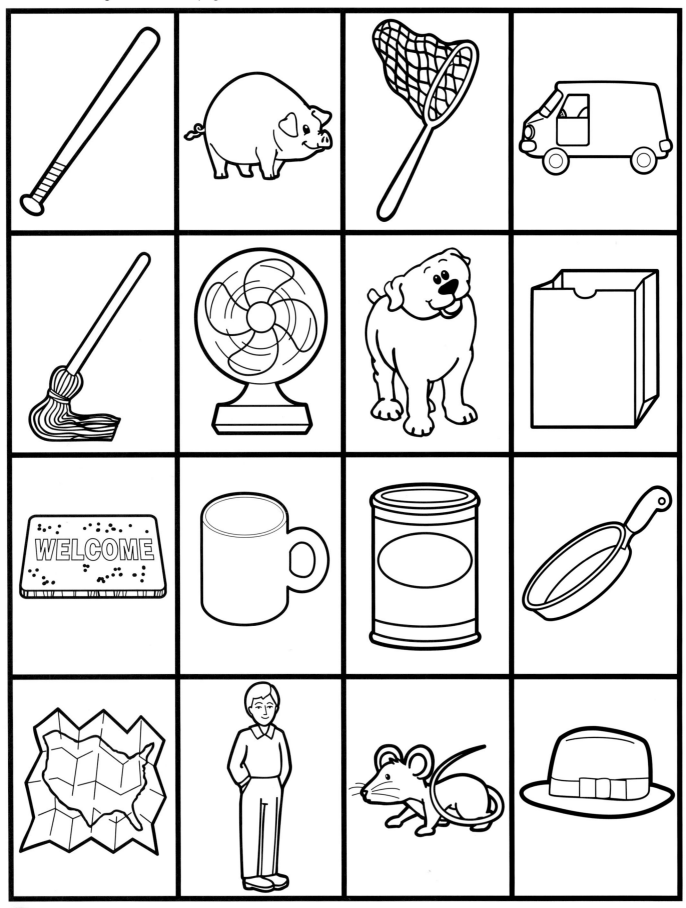

Name _____

Allie the Alligator

Color.

Cut.

Glue pictures whose names have a middle sound like 🥫.

©The Mailbox® • Storytime From A to Z • TEC60878

Note to the teacher: Use with "A-a-alligator Armor" on page 5.

7

B Is for Barnyard!

Barnyard Banter
Written and Illustrated by Denise Fleming

All the barnyard animals are sounding off, but where is Goose? Follow Goose throughout the story as he chases a butterfly across the barnyard and beyond!

Roll Call Banter
Using prior knowledge

Moo, moo, cluck, cluck, cock-a-doodle-doo! The barnyard animals noisily check in with this listening activity. In advance, make an enlarged red construction paper copy of the barn pattern on page 10. Cut out the barn and place it in the middle of your circle-time area. Gather a collection of plastic animals, including farm animals, and place them beside the barn. Show students the book cover and read the title aloud. Discuss the word *banter* with youngsters; then invite them to tell what they think might happen in the story. Next, help youngsters sort the farm animals from the collection as you name each one. Then make the sound of one farm animal as youngsters listen. Invite a student to name the animal that makes the sound and then place the corresponding toy animal on the barn cutout.

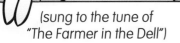

Barnyard Buzz
Recalling story events

The barnyard will be buzzin' as youngsters perform this movement activity similar to the familiar Farmer in the Dell game. Review the story illustrations with youngsters and encourage them to name the farm animals. Then have students stand in a circle and choose one child to stand in the center as the cow. Lead the group in singing the first verse of the song. Encourage youngsters to recall and name the next animal that appears in the story as a different child enters the center of the circle. Then sing the second verse. Repeat the second verse of the song, replacing the underlined words with a different animal and its sound as students recall from the story. Be sure to keep singing until each child has had a turn standing inside the circle!

(sung to the tune of "The Farmer in the Dell")

The cow's in the pasture,
The cow's in the pasture,
Moo, moo, moo, moo, moo.
The cow's in the pasture.

The [cow] sees the [rooster].
The [cow] sees the [rooster].
[Cock-a-doodle-doodle doo],
The [cow] sees the [rooster].

Bell Ringer
Recognizing the /b/ sound

Your little ones will want to play this small-group game until the cows come home! Gather a collection of objects, including items that begin with the /b/ sound, and several bells (cowbells if possible). Have your group sit in a circle, and give several different youngsters a bell to hold. Secretly place one object inside a paper bag. Review the /b/ sound with students and have them repeat the sound they hear at the beginning of *bell*. Then offer clues about the object in the bag. When a child guesses the name of the object, pull it out of the bag. Encourage each child to to ring her bell if the object begins with the /b/ sound. Repeat the activity with the remaining objects. Periodically invite a different child to be a bell ringer. Later, reinforce the /b/ sound by helping each child complete a copy of page 11.

Barnyard Buddies
Writing

Guess which animal buddy belongs in this barn! Practice writing and thinking skills as youngsters create clues about their secret barnyard animals. To prepare, make a red construction paper copy of the barn pattern on page 10 for each child. Give each child a 12" x 18" sheet of construction paper. Have her cut out her barn and then glue its top section onto the paper to create a flap as shown. Next, have each child cut out a magazine picture of a farm animal. Have her glue the picture onto the paper underneath the barn flap. Then help her write (or dictate as you write) clues to describe her animal as shown. Later, bind the completed pages between student-made covers to make a book. Then read the book to the class and encourage them to guess each barnyard buddy.

I have 4 legs.
I run fast.
I have a mane.
People ride me.
Who am I?

Alex

Barnyard Buddies

Barn Pattern

Use with "Roll Call Banter" on page 8 and "Barnyard Buddies" on page 9.

Name _____

Barnyard *B*s

🖍 Color.

✂ Cut.

Glue the pictures that begin with *b*.

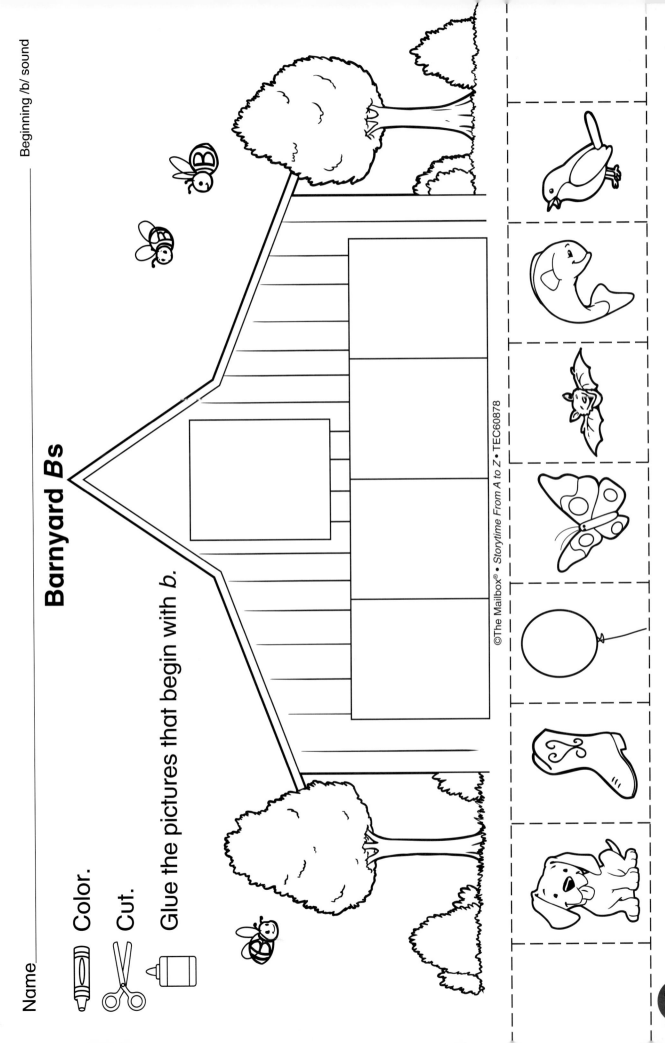

©The Mailbox® • *Storytime From A to Z* • TEC60878

C Is for Caterpillar!

The Very Hungry Caterpillar
Written and Illustrated by Eric Carle

Strawberries! Oranges! Chocolate cake! Throughout the week this voracious little caterpillar consumes a great quantity of unusual foods. Suddenly the caterpillar is no longer little, and he's ready for the next stage in his life!

Picture This!
Understanding metamorphosis

Before reading the story, help youngsters understand one of Mother Nature's amazing tricks—a caterpillar's metamorphosis! Color and then laminate a copy of page 14. Cut out the cards and prepare them for flannelboard use. While placing the cards on the flannelboard in sequence, explain each stage pictured. Then mix up the cards and have youngsters help reorder them. Finally, explain that the book you're about to read is about a caterpillar that eats some very unusual items before forming a chrysalis. Then have little ones listen to this fun read-aloud!

A butterfly lays eggs on a leaf.

The caterpillar forms a chrysalis.

A caterpillar hatches. It eats leaves.

The caterpillar is now a butterfly.

Seven Day Smorgasbord
Participating in a read-aloud

With this animated second reading, youngsters can see a week's worth of caterpillar cuisine! In advance, label separate large index cards with a different day of the week. Draw on a separate small index card each food item in the story. (For example, each pear should be drawn on its own card.) Cut from green construction paper a small caterpillar shape. Directly before the activity, ready several pieces of tape for student use. To begin, have youngsters help sequence the cards that show the days of the week as you tape them in a row on the board. Then give each child a food card. As you read the story, tape the caterpillar under the Sunday card to show the day it was born. Then, when indicated in the story, prompt each student to tape his card under the appropriate day. (Plan to tape any cards that are not represented by a child.) After the read-aloud, review the days of the week and orally count the number of food items under each day. If desired, remove the tape from the cards and place them and the book in a center for independent practice!

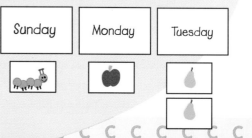

Sunday	Monday	Tuesday

C C C C C C C C C C C C C C C C C C C C C C C C C C C C C C C C C C

Cravings for C
Recognizing the hard C sound

Although the caterpillar in the story is not a finicky eater, the caterpillar in this activity only eats foods that begin with the hard C sound! Make a sock puppet that resembles a caterpillar. Also make a copy of page 15. Color, cut out, and laminate the picture cards. Then place the cards in a container. Next, don the sock puppet and have it choose a picture card. Say the name of the picture. If it begins with a hard C sound, prompt students to say, "Yes, please!" and have the sock puppet "devour" the card. If it doesn't begin with the hard C sound, prompt youngsters to say, "No thanks!" and have the puppet place the card in a separate pile.

More Munchies
Writing to complete a prompt

Why stop with the food in the book? With this activity, your youngsters complete a prompt to show the caterpillar's next food choice! For each child, program a sentence strip with the prompt "On ____ the caterpillar ate ____." Give each student a strip and have her complete the prompt by writing the name of a day and of a favorite food. Then encourage her to cut from appropriately colored construction paper a shape that resembles the food. If desired, have each student use crayons to further decorate the cutout. Next, have her draw a face on an end of a green construction paper strip. Then help her accordion-fold the strip to resemble a caterpillar. Encourage her to glue the caterpillar to the food cutout and then hole-punch around the edge of the cutout to show the area eaten. Display the sentence strips with their corresponding food items on a bulletin board or in a hallway display.

Metamorphosis Picture Cards
Use with "Picture This!" on page 12.

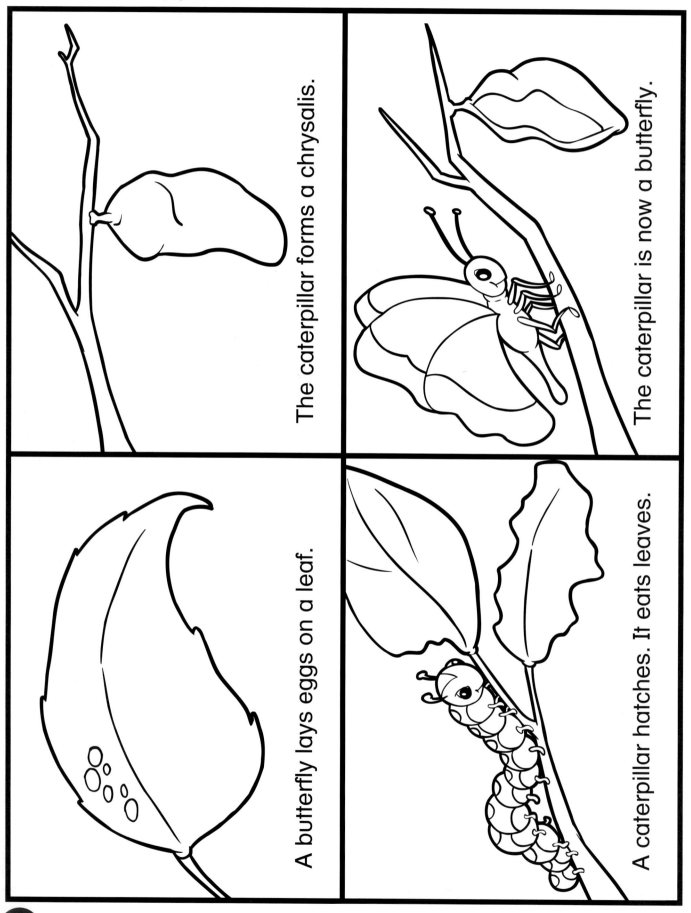

The caterpillar forms a chrysalis.

The caterpillar is now a butterfly.

A butterfly lays eggs on a leaf.

A caterpillar hatches. It eats leaves.

D Is for Ducklings!

Make Way for Ducklings
Written and Illustrated by Robert McCloskey

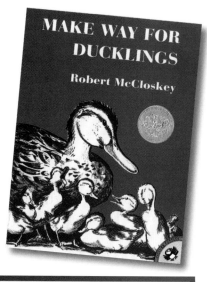

When Mr. and Mrs. Mallard's eight adorable ducklings hatch, they decide to relocate their family to Boston's Public Garden. A walk through the city's streets could be quite dangerous for a family of ducks. Fortunately for the Mallards, a friendly policeman helps them on their way, and they arrive safe and sound and ready to explore their wonderful new home.

Home, Sweet Home
Using prior knowledge

What can you tell me about a duck? Pose this question and others like it before reading the book, and youngsters are sure to eagerly share their opinions! After discussing responses to the question above, show students the front cover of the book and ask them where a duck might live. Lead students to the conclusion that a duck's home would need to be in a safe, warm place near water and food. Invite students to suggest what a duck's home might look like. Then, as you read the book, ask students to be on the lookout for the perfect home for the Mallards.

"Waddle" They Say?
Extending the text

What might a duckling say while walking down Boston's busy sidewalk? Your students will let you know when they make these chatty ducks! Duplicate page 19 onto white construction paper to make a class supply. Cut out each duck pattern. Gather a group of students in your art area. Give each child a duck cutout, a craft feather, and access to a shallow pan of yellow tempera paint. Invite each child to paint the duck cutout with the feather. Allow the paint to dry. Then have each youngster use a black marker to draw an eye on his duck.

Revisit the part of the story where the ducklings are walking along Boston's busy streets. Invite children to think about the ducklings' journey and how they may feel. Next, have each student dictate what a duckling might say as it waddles down a city street; write his words on a speech bubble similar to the one shown. Staple the ducks with their corresponding speech bubbles on a bulletin board titled "'Waddle' They Say?"

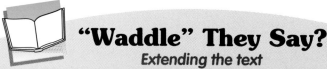

Quacking for *D*

Identifying words that begin with the /d/ sound

Youngsters are certain to say that this active game is just ducky! Cut from blue bulletin board paper a large pond shape and tape it to the floor in a traffic-free area of the room. Gather a small group of youngsters around the pond and say a word. If the word begins with the /d/ sound, encourage the youngsters to repeat the word while waddling onto the pond. Then have youngsters quack as they quickly waddle out of the pond. If the word does not begin with the /d/ sound, have them continue to stand outside the pond. After several rounds invite a new group of ducks to play the game.

Sack Rack Back Tack Jack Snack

A Pack of *-ack* Words

Identifying rhyming words

Youngsters will develop a knack for the *-ack* word family when they make this rhyming duckling parade. Copy page 19 onto yellow construction paper to make 12 to 16 ducks. Cut out each duck pattern. Write a different duckling's name from the story on each of eight cutouts. Then display them in a row on a wall or bulletin board. Keep the additional cutouts at hand. Next, read the names of the ducklings while pointing to each one. Ask students to identify the similarities between the names, leading them to the conclusion that all the names end with *-ack* and therefore rhyme. Explain that more ducks can be added to the parade but that they must also have names that end with *-ack*. Have students suggest new names for ducks as you write each one on a separate cutout and then add it to the row. It looks like Sack, Rack, Back, and Tack have joined the parade!

Quack, Quack, Hat!
Responding to literature through art

These darling duck hats are not only cute, but they're useful too! Use a reduced copy of the pattern on page 19 to make a duck template. Use the template to make two duck cutouts for each child. Also prepare a class supply of two-inch-wide tagboard headbands. Set up a painting area with sponges and yellow tempera paint. To make a hat, have a youngster place two duck cutouts face to face in the painting area and then sponge-paint both cutouts yellow. When the paint is dry, have him add beak, wing, and eye details with markers. To complete the hat, assist him in gluing the ducks near the middle of the headband as shown; then fit and staple the headband. Push a sheet of blue tissue paper into the inside of the hat and staple the edges to the headband to create a pond. Now have students don their hats and try one of the following extensions for added fun and learning.

- Have youngsters play a round of Duck, Duck, Goose while wearing their hats. The prop will add an interesting sound to the game.

- Brainstorm things that ducks would eat and make a list. Settle on a healthy selection from the list and gather the snacks. Take your little ones—with their hats—to a nearby duck pond or duck gathering place and have students feed the ducks. Videotape the adventure for later playback and discussion.

- Select students to act out *Make Way for Ducklings* as you read the text aloud.

Duckling Pattern

Use with "'Waddle' They Say?" on page 16, "A Pack of *-ack* Words" on page 17, and "Quack, Quack, Hat!" on page 18.

19

E Is for Egg!

Green Eggs and Ham
Written and Illustrated by Dr. Seuss

Do you like green eggs and ham? When Sam poses this question, it triggers a series of outlandish events designed to tempt the main character to try this colorful cuisine. The message of this rhyming tale is one children have undoubtedly heard before: You won't know if you like it until you try it!

Likes and Dislikes
Making a personal connection

No doubt all youngsters—and many adults—have eyed strange-looking foods with dislike! With this savory prereading activity, students can share some of their likes and dislikes with the class. To begin, present a hard-boiled egg with much fanfare and encourage youngsters to give a thumbs-up if they like eggs and a thumbs-down if they dislike eggs. Continue in this same fashion, naming other foods such as liver, spinach, or broccoli. Finally, ask students whether they have tasted the foods they dislike. After youngsters finish sharing their thoughts, explain that the story you're about to read has a character who is certain he dislikes a certain egg dish even though he has never tried it before. Then have children settle in for a reading of this wildly popular tale!

Ee

Eggs Up!
Associating the letter E with its sound

Help little ones develop "eggs-cellent" listening skills when they participate in a rereading of the story! In advance, make an egg cutout for each child and label it with an uppercase and a lowercase E. Gather students in your storytime area and give each child a prepared egg. As you read the story, prompt children to hold up their egg cutouts each time they hear the short E sound as in eggs. This is sure to be an "eggs-tra" special rereading!

E

On a Roll

Identifying words that contain the short E sound

Who wants to take a crack at this artsy learning opportunity? Your youngsters, that's who! For each child, prepare a large personalized *E* cutout. Place the cutout in a shallow box. Dunk a plastic egg in yellow paint and then place the paint-covered egg on the cutout. Encourage the child to roll the egg across the cutout by tilting the box. Then set the cutout aside to dry. Next, encourage students to suggest words that have the short *E* sound as you write their words on chart paper. Place the paper in a center along with a supply of colorful markers. A youngster visits the center with his prepared cutout in hand and then uses the chart as a reference to write words on his cutout that contain the short *E* sound. Excellent!

egg   elbow

bed

hen   mess   ten

leg

pet   net

Cracked Eggs

Identifying rhyming pictures

Mouse, house! Fox, box! Sound like fun? It sure is! Little ones match rhyming words with this playful partner activity. Color a copy of the egg patterns on page 23. Laminate the patterns for durability and then cut them apart. Place the cutouts at a center with six small paper plates. To begin, reread the book to your class, pausing for youngsters to supply each rhyming word. Invite a pair of students to the center. The students take turns choosing a puzzle piece, finding the picture with the rhyming name, and then placing the completed puzzle on a plate. That's one rhyming egg coming right up!

Creamy Eggs

Responding to literature through a craft

The eggs in this shaving cream craft look "eggs-actly" like the ones in the story! Make a mixture of equal parts shaving cream (nonmenthol) and white glue. To begin, show the cover of the book and have youngsters take notice of the picture of eggs with green yolks. Next, give each child a sheet of 12" x 18" green construction paper and a plastic spoon. Place several dollops of the prepared mixture on her paper. Then have her use the bowl of her spoon to spread each dollop to resemble the white of a fried egg. Encourage each youngster to cut green construction paper yolks from scrap paper and press one gently onto each egg white. Allow the project to dry for at least 48 hours. Then display the eggs on a wall in your classroom!

An Eggy Ballad

Responding to literature through a song

Youngsters are sure to enjoy singing this playful ditty about green eggs!

(sung to the tune of "I'm a Little Teapot")

I like my eggs scrambled, boiled, and fried.
Which one is best I just can't decide.
But if a bright green egg were served to me,
I would not like it, no sirree!

F Is for Fish!

Fish Eyes: A Book You Can Count On
Written and Illustrated by Lois Ehlert

Dive into a watery world and count from one to ten with schools of friendly fish! A guppy guide supplies simple addition facts throughout the book. But be careful—with all of these fun underwater antics, your youngsters just may wish they could be fish!

School of Students
Using prior knowledge

Engage little ones in this action-packed prereading activity, and they'll bubble over with excitement! Invite students to share what they know about fish. (You may wish to show photographs from nonfiction books as inspiration.) Then encourage students to pretend to be fish as they "swim" around the room. Invite them to change their movements, using words such as *jump, splash, dart,* and *dive.* Finally, have youngsters swim to your storytime area and sit down. Explain that the book you're about to read has many colorful fish doing what they do best. Then dive into the read-aloud!

A Splashy Sequence
Participating in a read-aloud, identifying numerals from 1 to 10

You can count on youngsters enjoying this vivid addition to a rereading of the story! Label each of ten large colorful fish cutouts with a different numeral from 1 to 10. To make the fish resemble the ones in the story, attach a hole reinforcer eye to each cutout as shown. Laminate the fish for durability. Then place them on a tabletop near your storytime area.

Begin reading the story. After reading each page that shows a numeral, invite a child to find the fish with the matching numeral. Encourage him to stand at the front of the room and hold up his fish to become part of the number line. When the story is finished and all ten fish are lined up in order, point to each fish as you count orally with your class. If desired, place the fish and book in a center for independent practice!

Catch of the Day
Identifying words that begin with the letter F

Youngsters help create a display that not only looks splashy but also provides an inspiring reference for writers! In advance, display a length of blue bulletin board paper with the title "Catch of the Day" near your large-group area. Make a supply of colorful fish cutouts. Next, revisit the book with your youngsters and have them identify words in the story that begin with the letter F, such as *fish*, *flip*, and *fin*. Write each word on a fish cutout and then attach each cutout to the paper. Continue in a similar fashion, having youngsters name other words that begin with the letter F as you add them to the display. Have students embellish the scene by gluing on paper seaweed, rocks, and seashells. When the glue is dry, attach the display to a wall in your writing center. When youngsters visit the center, encourage them to use the words on the display to create their own stories, labels, and lists. For practice with the /f/ sound, have children complete a copy of page 27.

Fancy Fish
Using descriptive words

Is this language activity fancy, flashy, or fun? Why, it's all of these things and more! Revisit the story, drawing students' attention to descriptive words such as *smiling*, *striped*, and *spotted*. Next, encourage each student to draw a fish on a 9" x 12" sheet of white construction paper. Have her decorate her fish by gluing on a variety of craft supplies such as glitter, wallpaper samples, and pieces of cellophane. Then have each child describe her fish as you write her words on the paper. When the projects are dry, bind them together in a class book titled "Our Fancy Fish."

My fish is green, yellow, shiny, and happy.

From Bag to Fish!
Responding to literature through art

Transform your classroom into an underwater wonderland with these three-dimensional fish! To begin, give each child a lunch-size paper bag and invite him to use crayons to decorate it as desired. Have him stuff the bag with newspaper. Then tie string around the open end to make a fish body and tail. Encourage each child to glue scraps of aluminum foil and construction paper to the fish to make fins, scales, eyes, and any other desired features. Finally, attach a paper clip to the top of the fish, as shown, to make a hanger. Then suspend the fish from your classroom ceiling. Now that's a school of fancy fish!

Swimming Song
Contributing to a song performance

This fun ditty is sure to make a splash with your little ones! When youngsters are comfortable singing the song, encourage them to add the motions provided.

(sung to the tune of "My Bonnie Lies Over the Ocean")

Oh, many fish live in the ocean.	*Ripple fingers to resemble waves.*
They swim in the water so blue.	*Pretend to swim.*
They jump, and they dart, and they frolic.	*Jump and pretend to swim playfully.*
Oh, wouldn't you like to swim too?	*Throw hands outward.*
Left fin, right fin,	*Wiggle left hand; wiggle right hand.*
Wiggle your tail fin—you're swimming free!	*Pretend to wiggle a tail fin.*
Left fin, right fin,	*Wiggle left hand; wiggle right hand.*
Just like the fish in the sea!	*Pretend to wiggle all fins.*

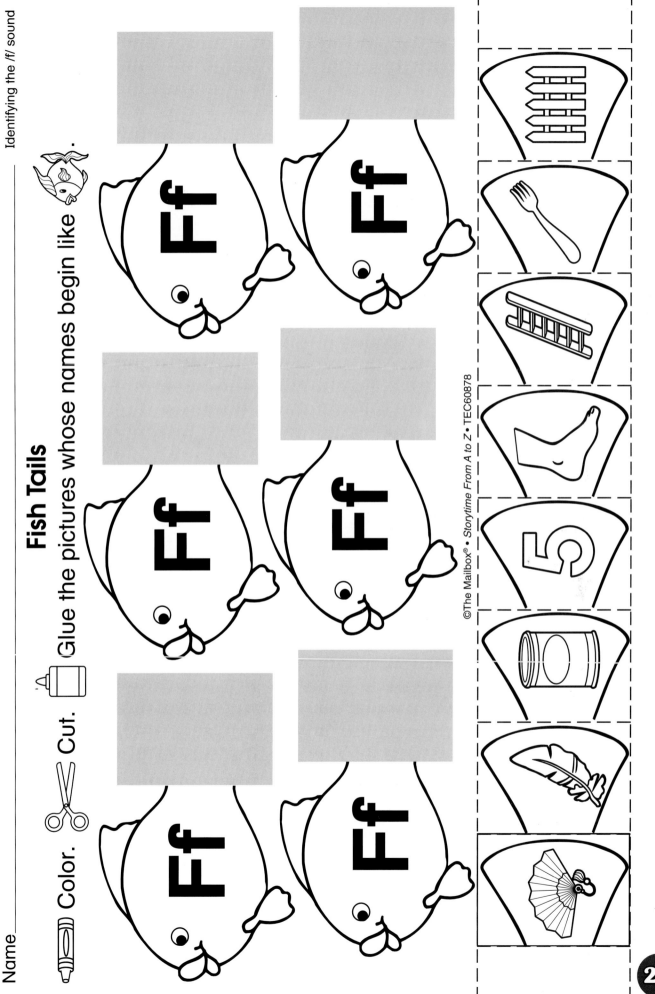

Name _____

Fish Tails

Glue the pictures whose names begin like .

Color. Cut.

©The Mailbox® • *Storytime From A to Z* • TEC60878

Note to the teacher: Use with "Catch of the Day" on page 25.

G Is for Gorilla!

Good Night, Gorilla
Written and Illustrated by Peggy Rathmann

A surprise is in store for a sleepy zookeeper's wife when a mischievous little gorilla steals the zookeeper's keys and opens the animal cages. Unknowingly, the zookeeper leads the animals home and into his bedroom where they all snuggle down for a good night's rest. His wife takes the animals back to the zoo, but guess who follows her home again?

Hide and Seek, Gorilla-Style!
Making a personal connection

Before reading the story, get youngsters excited about gorillas with a game of hide and seek. Hide a stuffed gorilla toy (or a picture of a gorilla) in your classroom. Place an empty, lidded box in your story area. Then gather students and announce that you have a special animal visitor. Dramatically open the box and look stunned that the animal is no longer inside. Explain that the escaped animal is playing a trick and you need students' help to find him. As you search the room together, give students clues about the gorilla, such as "He may be sitting on a shelf" or "He has two legs." When the gorilla is found, thank your little seekers for doing such a good job finding him and explain that this little guy doesn't stay where he should. Then settle youngsters down for a story about the gorilla's zoo adventures.

Dear Zookeeper,
    Did you know that the gorilla stole your keys? He let all the animals out of their cages. They followed you home. Your wife was scared! She took them back to the zoo. But the gorilla got out again. He ate a banana and then slept in your bed! We think you should put your keys around your neck so the gorilla can't get them anymore.

Your friends,
Brian
Remayja
Emma
Jae
Ella
Jack
Kamiya
Tiffany

Dear Mr. Zookeeper
Recalling story details

After a reading (and a good giggle), your little ones will be sure to discuss the gorilla's adventures! Invite students to recall story details while thinking of ways to tell the zookeeper about the animals' escape. When enough story details have been recalled, ask volunteers to dictate sentences as you write a letter to the zookeeper on a sheet of chart paper. Confirm the details and sequencing by repeating each sentence aloud before writing. End the letter with suggested ways to keep the animals safely confined. Enlist student help to read the completed letter aloud. Then have each child sign the letter. Bet the animals stay safely in the zoo from now on!

G

Gorilla Walk
Recognizing the hard G sound

Searching for hard G is more fun when you pretend to walk like a gorilla! In advance, invite students to look through old magazines and cut out pictures of objects whose names begin with the same sound as *gorilla*. Meanwhile, cut out several pictures of objects whose names begin with other consonant sounds. When you have a sizable collection, mount all the pictures on tagboard, laminate them if desired, and then tape them to the floor in an open area of your classroom. Direct students to say each picture name before stepping and to only walk on the pictures whose names start like *gorilla*. Then model walking like a gorilla as you name a few pictures, stepping only on those beginning with hard G. Then have each small group take a turn walking like a gorilla and naming the hard G pictures. For additional practice with the hard G sound, encourage each child to complete a copy of page 31. Good job, Gorilla!

ICE KREM

The gorilla wt to the ice Krem sty. He bt ice Krem cons. He ate 2.! DANA

Gorilla's Adventures
Creative writing

Continue the saga of the mischievous little gorilla with these exciting gorilla adventure displays. Give each child a sheet of colorful construction paper and have her fold it in half to make a standing display. Next, instruct her to think about the end of the story and decide what the gorilla will do the next time he escapes. Support her as needed as she writes a sentence or two describing the gorilla's next adventure. Then have her use crayons, markers, and assorted craft supplies to illustrate the outside of the display. Have students stand their completed displays on tabletops around the room. Invite volunteers to read their displays aloud for a giggle-filled peek into the little gorilla's future adventures!

Is There a Gorilla in My Bed?

Responding to literature through art

Tuck this gorilla into its cozy bed and your students will be eager to retell this popular story event. Just have each child follow the steps below. Then put the sleeping gorillas on display on a flat surface. Sleep tight, Gorilla!

Supplies:
9" x 12" sheet of white construction paper
washable black and gray paint
paintbrush
fine-tip black marker
scissors
9" x 15" wallpaper scrap
glue
4 cotton balls
two 3" x 4" pieces of tissue paper

Steps:
1. With your palm painted black, make a palm print in the middle of the white construction paper for the gorilla's body.
2. Make three overlapping black thumbprints for the head.
3. Paint arms and legs using one of your fingers.
4. Make gray thumbprints for the face and feet.
5. When the paint is dry, add facial details and hands with a fine-tip black marker.
6. Cut around the finished gorilla and write the child's name on the back. (teacher step)

Steps to make a bed:
1. Glue four cotton balls on the back of the wallpaper as shown.
2. Draw a line of glue around each set of cotton balls and press the tissue paper onto the glue to make two pillows.
3. Fold the paper up to just below the pillows.
4. Glue along the edges only, forming a pocket.
5. When the glue is dry, place the gorilla in the bed.

Name

Sweet Dreams

Find the pictures that begin like 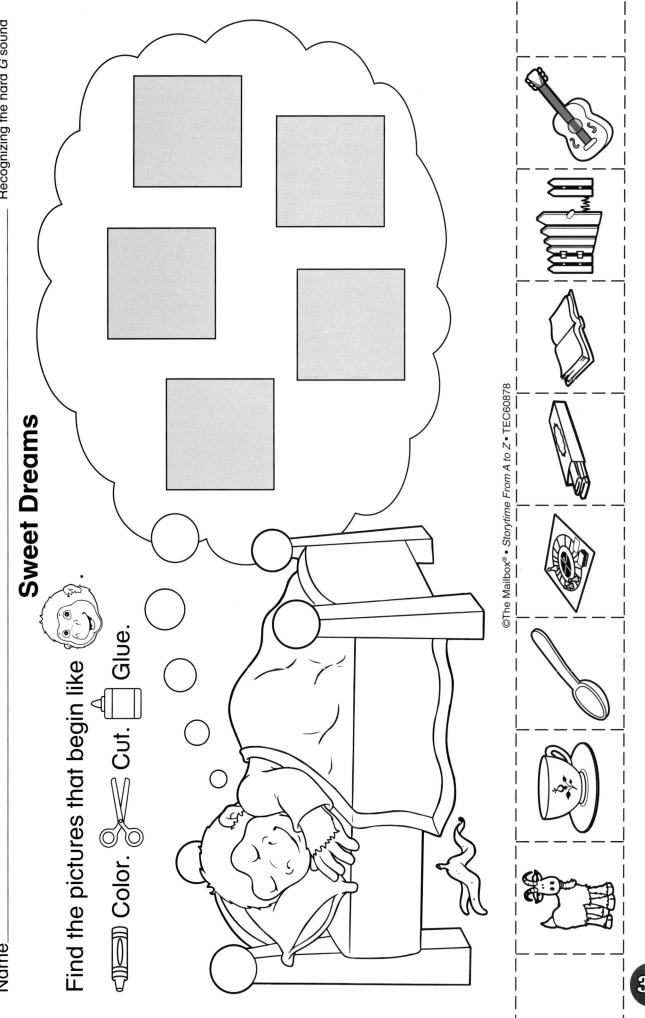 .

Color. Cut. Glue.

©The Mailbox® • *Storytime From A to Z* • TEC60878

Note to the teacher: Use with "Gorilla Walk" on page 39.

H Is for House!

A House for Hermit Crab
Written and Illustrated by Eric Carle

It's moving day for Hermit Crab! His shell is too tight, so he must find a larger one. When he moves into the perfect-size home, he notices the exterior is drab and unappealing. But this is no problem for Hermit Crab. The sea is full of friendly creatures happy to hitch a ride!

A Decorative House
Using prior knowledge

When you use youngsters' prior knowledge about houses to grab their attention, your storytime will go swimmingly! Before reading the story, draw the outline of a house on a sheet of chart paper. Have students suggest ways to embellish the house to make it look nice, such as drawing a colorful door or windows with curtains. After adding their suggestions to the drawing, ask if snails or starfish would make the house more attractive. When the giggles subside, explain that the story you're about to read has an animal that decorates its home with many unique items. Then have students settle in for this entertaining read-aloud!

Moving In
Exploring a character through role-playing

Expect a wave of excitement when youngsters choose and decorate a house just like Hermit Crab! Collect three different-size boxes to represent shells, making sure that only the large box is big enough for a child to sit in. After a second reading of the story, explain to your youngsters that they will pretend to be hermit crabs and the boxes will be shells. Place the boxes on their sides in a center. Over the next few days, encourage youngsters to visit the center to see which home fits them the best, reminding them that a hermit crab needs to completely fit inside its shell. Discuss which home is the best choice and then remove the two extra boxes. Provide craft supplies such as wallpaper samples, tissue paper, and construction paper scraps. Have youngsters cut out and decorate sea creatures and glue them to the bottom and exposed sides of the box. Now that's a house any crab would be proud of! For practice matching animals to their homes, have youngsters complete a copy of page 35.

House of Cards

Identifying words that begin with the /h/ sound

There's more than one way to decorate a house! Students decorate this supersize hermit crab home with words for an eye-catching writing reference! Make a large hermit crab shell from colorful bulletin board paper. Title it "Hermit Crab's Home" and display it in your large-group area. Encourage youngsters to listen carefully for the /h/ sound as you read the title aloud. Then have them suggest words that begin with the /h/ sound as you write each word on an index card. Invite students to tape the cards to the display. Move the display to a wall near your writing center for students to use as a reference for writing lists, labels, and stories. Hurray!

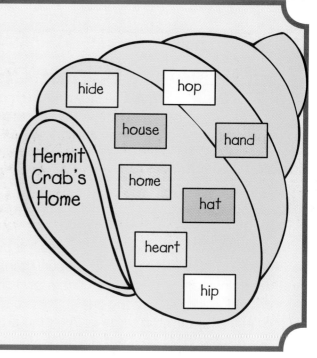

Hermit Crab's Home — hide, hop, house, hand, home, hat, heart, hip

Hermit Crab
111 Sandy Bottom
The Ocean, Earth 12345

Shana Brown
1234 Any Road
Anytown, NC 45678

Where Do You Live?

Developing an awareness of own address

When you present this amusing comparison to your youngsters, they're sure to understand that every home has an address! For each child, fold a 12" x 18" sheet of white construction paper in half. Unfold it and label one half of the paper with an invented address for Hermit Crab and label the remaining half with the youngster's address. Next, explain that people need addresses so others can find where they live and so they can receive mail. Read Hermit Crab's address. Have each student draw a picture of Hermit Crab's home above the address. Then encourage each child to draw a picture of her own home above his address. Finally, have each youngster take her paper home to practice saying her address with her parents.

Traveling Hermit Crab

Responding to literature through art

With a house on its back, a hermit crab is packed and ready to travel! Invite little ones to show a hermit crab's travels through the sand with this crafty project. Have each youngster draw a picture of a hermit crab and then cut it out. Next, encourage her to brush a mixture of sand and light brown tempera paint on a sheet of 12" x 18" white construction paper. Invite her to glue her prepared hermit crab to a corner of the paper. Then, while the paint is still wet, have her use a craft stick to draw a trail, similar to the one shown, to show-case the hermit crab's travels. After the projects are dry, display them on a bulletin board titled "Happy Trails!"

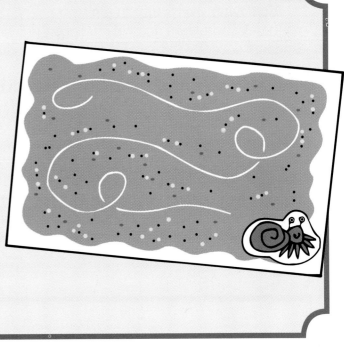

A Decorated Crab

Reviewing story events

Little ones really come out of their shells for this musical review of the story! Revisit the story with your youngsters and then lead them in singing the song.

(sung to the tune of "Twinkle, Twinkle, Little Star")

In a shell lives Hermit Crab.
His home looks a little drab.
He adds creatures from the sea,
Like a small anemone.
Add a snail and coral too
And a small starfish in blue.

When he grows out of his shell,
He bids all his friends farewell.
He will find a bigger place,
One that has a lot of space.
Time to decorate once more
With friends from the ocean floor!

Home, Sweet Home

 Color. ✂ Cut. Glue.

A hermit crab's home is a shell.

A rabbit's home is a burrow.

A bird's home is a nest.

A bear's home is a den.

©The Mailbox® • *Storytime From A to Z* • TEC60878

I Is for Itsy!

The Itsy Bitsy Spider
Written and Illustrated by Iza Trapani

Inspire youngsters to think about itsy-bitsy things as they follow the irresistible itsy-bitsy spider through this adventurous story. The beautiful artwork allows students to compare the itsy-bitsy spider to her much larger surroundings as she finds just the right spot to spin a web.

Up the Waterspout
Introducing new vocabulary

What is a waterspout? Is it itsy or great big? Use this fun activity to help youngsters visualize the itsy-bitsy spider's journey up and down the spout. Give each child a plastic spider ring and a flexible plastic drinking straw to represent a waterspout. Before reading the book, sing "The Itsy-Bitsy Spider" with youngsters. Guide each child to slide her spider up and down her waterspout as she sings the song again. Then show your group the illustration of the waterspout in the book. Are their waterspouts itsy or great big? Challenge them to think of other ways to use their waterspouts and spiders (such as pouring water into the straw to wash the spider down). Incredible fun!

Web Weavin'
Recalling story events

The itsy-bitsy spider would be proud of this great big story web! Have your group sit in a circle and read the story to them. Next, show them a ball of yarn and tell them they will help spin a web by answering questions about the story. Ask the student seated across from you to name one place the itsy-bitsy spider climbs. If she correctly recalls a place, hold the loose end of the yarn and roll the ball to her to begin the web. Continue in this manner until each child has recalled a story fact. Then have youngsters look at the web they have woven and encourage them to compare it to the itsy-bitsy spider's web.

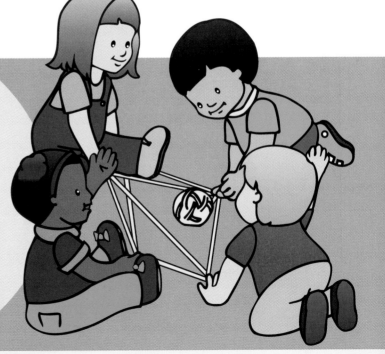

Itsy *I* Words
Recognizing the short I sound

This eight-legged display will help youngsters recognize words that begin with short *I*. To prepare, cut out a large spider body and head from colored construction paper, as shown. Display the partial spider on a wall. Then give each child an appropriate newspaper section to search for words that begin with *I*. Ask each youngster to find and circle several words. Later, gather your group and help students share some of their words with the class. Next, tell youngsters that some of their words will help complete the itsy-bitsy spider on the wall. Then have students help find the itsy words that begin with short *I*, such as *in*, *is*, *it*, and *if*. Write each word on a separate index card. Invite different students to tape each card onto the spider to represent her eight legs. Then review the words again with the class.

if   its

in   icky

it   ill

is   into

My
Itsy Book

by ___Caleb___

Itsy Booklet
Identifying size

Itty-bitty, teeny-weeny, tiny—there are lots of ways to say *itsy*! Ask youngsters to name things that are itsy-bitsy. Record their ideas on a chart. Give each child a copy of pages 38 and 39; read the text aloud. Have him name the itsy-bitsy objects pictured on the cards. Then have him write his name on the cover and then color and cut apart the booklet pages and picture cards. Ask him to glue the picture cards in the spaces provided on booklet pages 1–5. Have him draw a picture of a different itsy-bitsy object on booklet page 6. Help him sequence the pages and then staple them together along the left side. Later, invite partners to read their booklets to each other.

My Itsy Book

by _____

A seashell is itsy.

1

A ladybug is too.

2

A button is itsy.

3

A snowflake is too.

4

A spider is itsy.

5

See the itsy things
I drew.

6

J Is for Jam!
Jamberry
Written and Illustrated by Bruce Degen

A little boy and a bear frolic through a whimsical land where they look for tasty berries for jam! The rhyming story follows the characters as they cavort through a jam-filled land featuring strawberry sheep, raspberry rabbits, and many other playful critters! Your little ones will devour this fun selection!

Berry Ballot
Building prior knowledge, graphing

Before reading the story, engage student interest with a "berry" pleasing taste test! In advance, prepare a supply of black and red berry-shaped cutouts (blackberries and raspberries). Also make a simple two-column floor graph out of bulletin board paper. Title each column as shown. Then place the floor graph in your storytime area. To begin, invite each student to sample a small amount of raspberry and blackberry jam on crackers. Have each child determine which jam he prefers. Then encourage him to choose a corresponding cutout and place it in the appropriate column on the graph. As a class, count the number of berries in each column. Have youngsters compare the numbers using words such as *more* and *less*. Next, explain that the book selection for storytime is about blackberry jam, raspberry jam, and other kinds of jam as well. Then have youngsters listen to this fantastical read-aloud!

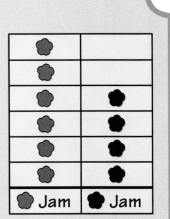

Suggested Rhymes
blueberry: *shoeberry, canoeberry, mooberry, glueberry, chewberry, zooberry*
strawberry: *gnawberry, drawberry, pawberry, sawberry, rawberry, thawberry*

A Jam Session
Identifying rhyming words

Spoon up a serving of rhyming practice with this unique small-group activity. In advance, make two large jar cutouts in the colors shown. Label the blue jar "blueberry" and the red jar "strawberry." Make several white construction paper copies of the spoon patterns on page 42. Label each spoon handle with a rhyming word from the suggestions given. Laminate the spoons. Place the prepared items at a table. Then reread the book to your class, leading youngsters to notice the rhyming words such as *pawberry* and *strawberry*. Gather a small group of students at the table and have a child choose a spoon. Read the word; then encourage her to decide which berry rhymes with the word given. Have her place the spoon on the corresponding jam jar. Continue in a similar fashion, having youngsters take turns until each spoon has been placed on a jar. Finally, prompt youngsters to identify words on the spoons that are also in the story. Shoeberry, canoeberry, blueberry!

jump!

Jam
Jar

J Is for Jam
Associating the letter J with /j/

Little ones will jam this jar full of play dough berries to show their knowledge of the /j/ sound. Label a small plastic jar as shown and place it at a table with a container full of red play dough balls (berries). Invite two youngsters to the table. Revisit the cover of the book and have students identify the letter *J* in *Jamberry*. Next, say a familiar word to one of the students and have her indicate whether it begins with /j/. If it does, invite the child to place a berry in the jam jar. Continue in the same way, having the youngsters take turns. When the jam jar is full, encourage the students to count the berries as you place them back in the container. For additional letter-sound association practice, have each youngster complete a copy of page 43.

JAM

P am

j

h

s y

r

Jam, Yam, Ham
Building words that belong to the –am family

Will youngsters enjoy building words from the *-am* word family? Yes, ma'am! In advance, draw a jam jar on copy paper and then make a class supply. Label a blue construction paper jar cutout as shown. Also label each of six blueberry cutouts with a different letter from the following list: *j, h, y, P, S,* and *r*. Place the items at a table in a center along with red, blue, and purple markers. A child visits the center, chooses a blueberry, and places it on the jar cutout to make a word. She then sounds out the word and uses a marker to write it on a copy of the jam jar. She repeats the process with each blueberry. Then she takes her completed paper home to share with her family.

Alicia

Sam   Pam

jam

ham

yam

ram

"Berry" Special Painting

Responding to literature through art

Berry jam is the inspiration for these colorful art projects! Obtain jars of strawberry, blueberry, and raspberry jam (or gather pictures of each kind of jam). Gather a small group of children in your art area and present the jars of jam with much fanfare. Have them describe the color of each kind of jam. Next, give each child a 12" x 18" sheet of tan construction paper. Have each youngster brush on his paper purple, light red, and dark red tempera paint—the same colors as blueberry, strawberry, and raspberry jam! Then have him use a plastic knife to make designs in the paint until a desired effect is achieved. When the project is dry, trim each paper to resemble a bread slice. Then display the finished projects in your classroom!

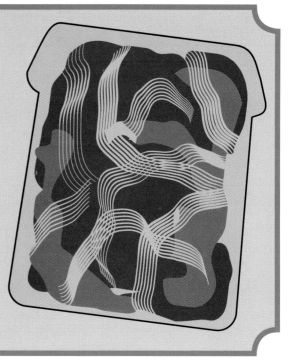

Spoon Patterns
Use with "A Jam Session" on page 40.

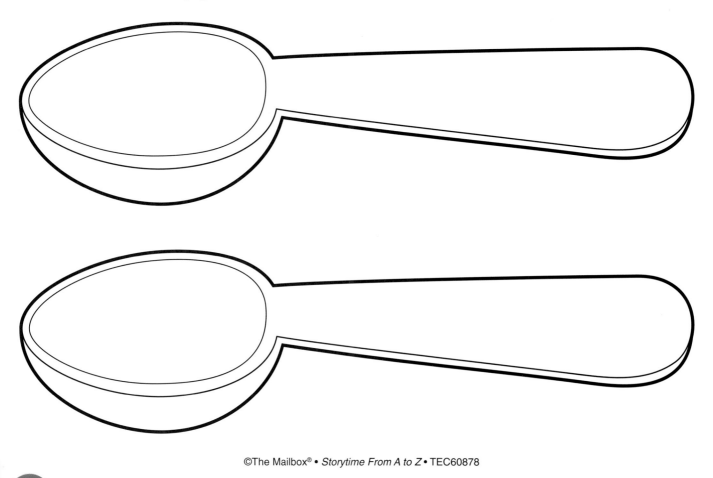

Name _____

Jam Jars

Color the pictures whose names begin like .

Bonus Box: Write each *J* word on the back of this sheet.

Note to the teacher: Use with "*J* Is for *Jam*" on page 41.

K Is for Kindergarten!

Miss Bindergarten Gets Ready for Kindergarten

Written by Joseph Slate
Illustrated by Ashley Wolff

It's the first day of kindergarten, and Miss Bindergarten is busy, busy, busy preparing an inviting classroom for 26 new students. At the same time, each cute kindergarten character is getting ready in his or her own way for the big day. When the kindergartners meet Miss Bindergarten, they know that school will be cool!

Kindergarten Prep
Predicting

How does a teacher get a classroom ready for kindergartners? Ask youngsters what they think was done to prepare the classroom for them. Offer some examples of things that need to be done before school begins, such as setting up centers or shelving books. Then show students the book cover and ask them to predict what the teacher might do with the objects she is carrying. As you read the story aloud, challenge each child to observe how an item pictured on the cover is used to prepare the classroom. Afterward, discuss students' predictions. Were they accurate?

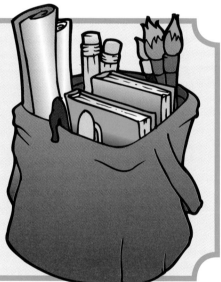

It's Time to Rhyme
Identifying rhyming words

Youngsters are sure to say that all the cuddly characters in this story get ready for school in a rhyming way. Review with students several pages in the story and point out the rhyming words on each page. Next, reread the story, stopping periodically to observe the illustrations, and challenge youngsters to repeat the rhyming words. Then, to reinforce rhyming pictures, have each child complete a copy of page 46.

Catch That K!
Recognizing the letter K

Kiki and the cast of characters from the story challenge youngsters to catch all the letter K names in this center activity. To prepare, label a separate index card with each character's name. Place at a center the cards and a basket labeled with the letter K. Ask a pair of students to look at each card. Have the students sort out all the cards with names that contain the letter K and place those cards in the basket. Next, have them count the number of Ks they caught. Then have them empty the basket and mix up the cards for the next pair of students.

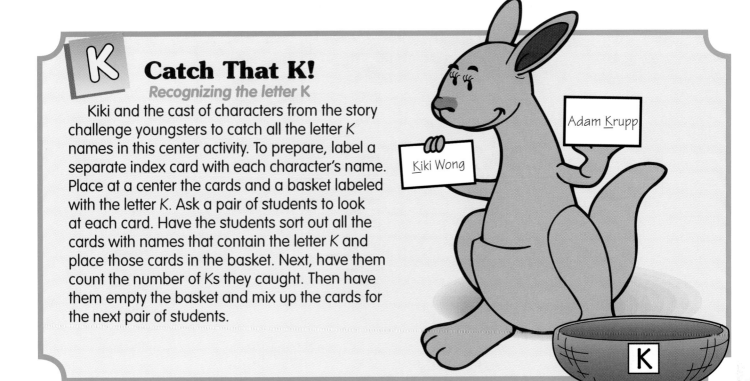

Kiki Wong

Adam Krupp

K

All Ready
Writing to complete a sentence

How do you get ready for the first day of kindergarten? Every child will have a chance to tell his story with this sentence starter activity. In advance, make a class supply of page 47. Discuss with students what they did to get ready for the first day of kindergarten. Give each child a copy of the sheet and then read the sentence starter aloud. Next, help each child write or dictate to complete the sentence. Ask him to illustrate his sentence. When all students have finished, stack the pages between two covers and staple the book together along the left side. Read the book to your group and then place it at a center for all to enjoy.

Mrs. Kelly's Class Gets Ready for Kindergarten

On the first day of kindergarten, I eat brekfst.

Name

K Classroom

Color.

Cut.

Glue to match rhyming pictures.

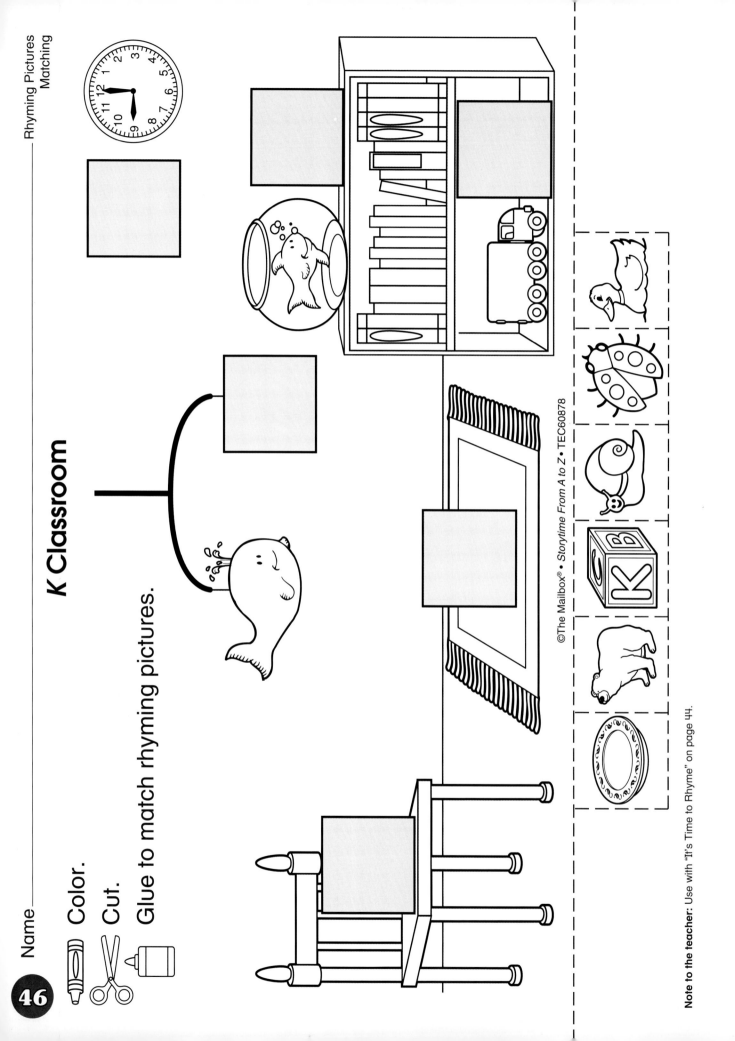

©The Mailbox® • *Storytime From A to Z* • TEC60878

46

Note to the teacher: Use with "It's Time to Rhyme" on page 44.

Name _____

On the first day of kindergarten, I _____.

Note to the teacher: Use with "All Ready" on page 45.

L Is for Lunch!

Lunch
Written and Illustrated by Denise Fleming

Red apples! Purple grapes! Yellow corn! Join a ravenous rodent for his lunchtime romp through a smorgasbord of colorful foods. Don't forget to look at the final page, where each food remnant clinging to the mouse's fur is labeled for a rib-tickling color-word review!

Colorful Cuisine
Building color-word recognition

Ask youngsters to draw their favorite lunchtime food for this color activity, and they're sure to be "berry" pleased! Draw several large circles on your board and label each one with a different color word. Ask each student to name her favorite lunchtime food. Then encourage her to draw on a large sticky note the food in the appropriate color. When each student is finished, have her bring her note to the board and stick it in the corresponding circle. (If there is more than one color on the child's drawing, encourage her to choose the color that is the most prominent.) Finally, explain to students that the character in the book you're about to read likes a colorful lunch just as much as they do! Then watch youngsters gobble up this fun read-aloud.

Multicolored Mice
Recalling story details

Youngsters may use a sponge to clean up lunchtime spills, but this recall activity uses sponges to re-create the mouse's mess! For each color represented in the story, place a thin layer of tempera paint in a shallow pan. Place the pans at your art table along with a nylon bath puff for each one. To begin, revisit the book with your youngsters, encouraging them to name the foods the mouse eats for lunch. Invite one or more students to the table and give each child a 12" x 18" sheet of gray construction paper. Have him use the sponges to cover the paper with colorful prints. As he paints each color, prompt him to recall the corresponding food. Allow time for the paint to dry. Then, on each paper, trace a mouse shape similar to the one shown. Have each student cut out his mouse. Then encourage him to use paper scraps to add legs, a tail, and any other desired features. These critters may not be squeaky clean, but they'll look great displayed in your classroom!

A Memorable Meal

Recognizing words that begin with the /l/ sound

Help little ones digest the /l/ sound with a few rounds of this lunchbox memory activity! In advance, obtain a lunchbox and make a copy of page 50. Color, cut apart, and laminate the cards. Then prepare each one for flannelboard use. As you present each card to your youngsters, have them repeat the picture's name while listening carefully for the /l/ sound. Then place the pictures on your flannelboard. Encourage students to close their eyes as you remove a picture and place it inside the lunchbox. Invite them to open their eyes and name the missing picture. When they guess correctly, open the lunchbox and reveal the picture. Continue in the same way, removing a different picture each time. For an extra challenge, rearrange the pictures on the flannelboard every few rounds! For more practice with the letter *L*, have each youngster complete a copy of page 51.

A Lovely Lunch

Potluck Lunch

Identifying words that begin with the same letter

Paper plates make perfect pages for this lunch-themed class book! Help each child think of a food item whose name begins with the first letter in her name (using a matching sound if possible). Program a large paper plate, as shown, substituting the child's name and food choice. Encourage each student to draw a picture of the food on the paper plate. To make a cover for the book, label a plate with the title "A Lovely Lunch." Hole-punch the cover and pages, stack them with the cover on top, and then bind them together with a metal ring. After reading the book aloud to your class, place it in your independent reading center. Pass the plate book, please!

Hannah brought a hamburger.

Picture Cards

Use with "A Memorable Meal" on page 49.

lemon

lollipop

lemonade

licorice

lettuce

lime

lima beans

lasagna

What's for Lunch?

Color.

Circle the foods whose names begin like ▦.

Lunch

Ms. Sour's Lemonade

Bonus Box: On the back of this sheet, draw and label what you like to eat for lunch.

©The Mailbox® • *Storytime From A to Z* • TEC60878

Note to the teacher: Use with "A Memorable Meal" on page 49.

M Is for Mud!

Mud
Written by Mary Lyn Ray
Illustrated by Lauren Stringer

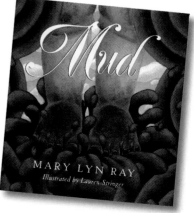

When winter melts away into spring, it often leaves a legacy of sticky, squishy, slurpy mud! Youngsters of all ages will enjoy this beautifully illustrated story about the mud that brings the fresh green of spring.

Signs of Spring
Using prior knowledge

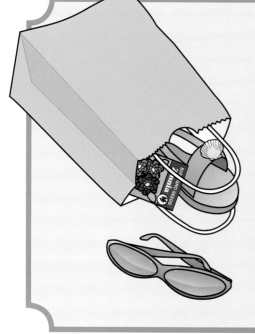

Prior to reading this springtime story, play this musical circle-time game with your youngsters! To prepare, put a variety of spring items into an opaque bag. (Items could include seed packets, sunglasses, artificial grass, a baseball glove, and sandals.) Gather youngsters and teach them this quick ditty sung to the tune of "Short'nin' Bread."

Spring is in the air. Spring is coming!
Spring is in the air. Spring, spring, spring!

While students sing the song, have them pass the bag around the circle. At the end of the song, have the child holding the bag remove one item. Then encourage the child to identify the item and tell how it relates to springtime. Repeat the activity until the bag is empty. Then introduce the book and explain to students that the muddy cover illustration makes some people think of springtime.

Come, Spring, Come!
Developing story comprehension

After reading, dig a little deeper into this tale to create an easy-to-read comprehension chart. Write "Come, _____" several times on a chart. Then ask students to think about the story. Fill in some of the blanks on the chart as they name things from the story that came as spring did, such as thaw, grass, green, and mud. As a class, discuss why those things signal spring's arrival, especially mud. Then discuss spring's arrival in your area. Does the frozen ground thaw, leaving mud behind? Does lots of rain fall, creating mud? Return to the chart and write to complete the remaining blanks as volunteers name spring signals that are unique to your area. Conclude the activity by writing "Come, spring!" and then rereading the chart with your youngsters. Sounds like spring has arrived!

Come, _thaw_ .
Come, _mud_ .
Come, _grass_ .
Come, _green_ .
Come, _flowers_ .
Come, _sun_ .
Come, _butterflies_ .
Come, spring!

M-m-marvelous M-m-mud
Recognizing the beginning sound /m/

Jump into this neat and clean mud puddle game to reinforce the /m/ sound! To prepare, cut a large mud puddle shape from brown poster board. Copy page 55 onto white construction paper. Color and cut out the picture cards; then laminate them for durability if desired. To play, two students sit on opposite sides of the mud puddle cutout. They stack the cards. One child draws a card and names the picture. If it is an object whose name begins with /m/, she places the card on her side of the mud puddle. If the object's name begins with another sound, she places it beside the mud puddle. Then her partner draws and identifies the next card. Play continues until the cards run out. Does mouse begin like mud? Yes, it does!

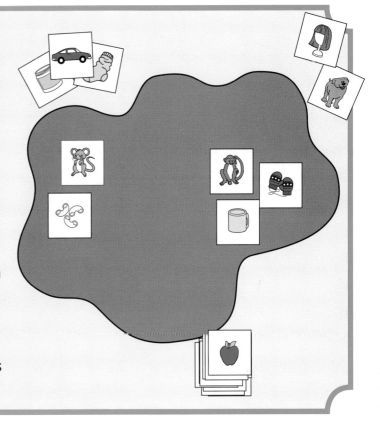

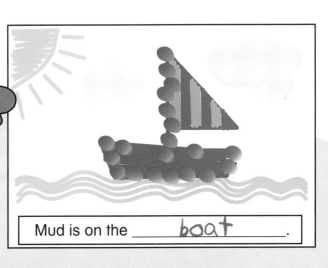

Mud is on the ___boat___.

Mud Is Everywhere!
Writing to complete a sentence

Don't worry—it's really just brown fingerpaint! Inspire some creative writing with mud in mind. In advance, glue a sentence starter strip (page 54) to the bottom of a sheet of drawing paper as shown. Prepare a sheet for each child and place the sheets at an art center along with brown finger-paint and pencils. When each child visits this center, help him read the prompt and then write to complete the sentence. Next, have him illustrate the page and then dab brown fingerpaint on the illustration to resemble mud. Bind the dried pages into a class book titled "Mud Is Everywhere!"

A Mud Dance
Developing gross-motor skills

No doubt your little ones will love this squishy, muddy, outdoor activity! In advance, position a long length of light-colored bulletin board paper on the ground. Prepare a batch of mud in a container large enough for a student to step in. Place the container beside one end of the paper. At the opposite end of the paper, partially fill a kiddie pool with water and a small amount of liquid soap. Also provide towels to dry wet feet.

To begin, have youngsters take off their shoes. Play some music and encourage students to dance. Invite each child, in turn, to step into the mud and then onto the paper. Encourage him to dance his way to the other end of the paper. After each child has had a chance to dance and the paper has dried, add the title "Memories of Our Mud Dance" and display it for everyone to see.

Sentence Starter Strips
Use with "Mud Is Everywhere!" on page 53.

Mud is on the _____.
Mud is on the _____.
Mud is on the _____.

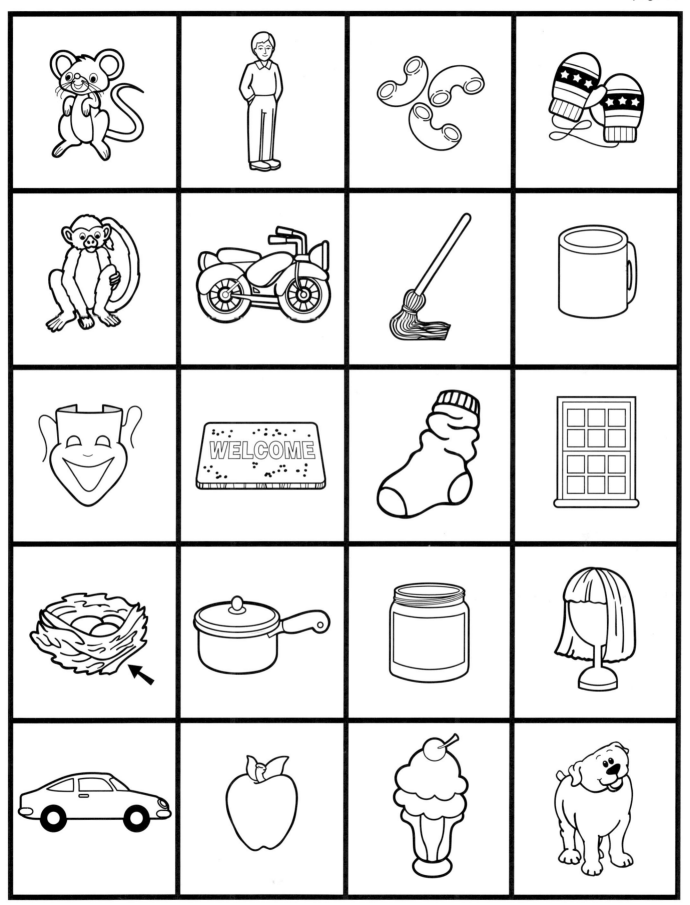

N Is for Naps!

The Napping House
Written by Audrey Wood
Illustrated by Don Wood

As rain pours down, a child, a dog, a cat, and a mouse crawl on a bed to take a nap with a granny. But when a tiny flea hops on the pile, everyone's peaceful slumber comes to an end! Giggle-inducing illustrations are sure to prompt youngsters to ask for a rereading of this cumulative story!

The Sound of Silence
Developing listening skills

Naptime is quiet time! Before reading the book, have little ones take a pretend nap to find out how quiet the room can be when everyone is sleeping. Encourage little ones to lie down and be as quiet as possible while they pretend to nap. After several seconds, have students sit up. Then ask them to share any sounds they heard that normally aren't noticed, such as the heater running, the clock ticking, or other students breathing. Next, explain that the book you're about to read is about a quiet napping house that ends up having quite a ruckus. Then have little ones tune in to this playful tale.

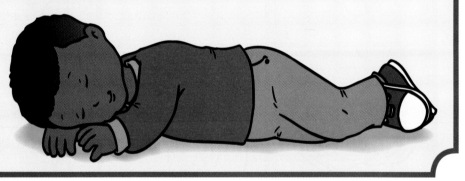

Stack Them Up!
Retelling story events

Turn your block center into a napping house with these storytelling props. Make or gather pictures to represent the following items and characters in the story: bed, granny, child, dog, cat, mouse, and flea. Laminate the pictures and then tape each one to a block. After a second reading of the book, place the blocks and the book in your block center. Children can re-create the story by stacking the blocks, using the book for a reference if needed. Uh-oh! There goes the flea on top!

Naptime!

Identifying words that begin with the /n/ sound

Spotlight the /n/ sound with this engaging activity, and youngsters will never look at naptime the same way again! Enlarge a copy of the picture cards (page 58). Then color and cut out the cards. Present a card and say the name of the picture. If the name begins with the /n/ sound, youngsters lie down and pretend to take a nap. If the name of the picture begins with a different sound, the students remain awake. Continue in the same way with each picture card. These naps won't take the place of your youngsters' regular naptime, but they sure are filled with learning fun!

Who Naps?

by _Doug_

Numerous Nappers

Writing simple sentences

Who takes a nap? Many people and animals do. Have youngsters spotlight nappers with this simple booklet. For each child, make a copy of the cover and booklet pages on page 59. Have him write his name on the cover and decorate it as desired. Then encourage each youngster to think of a person or animal that naps. Have him draw a picture of the person or animal on the first page of the booklet. Encourage each child to complete the sentence to tell who is napping. Then have him repeat the process for each remaining booklet page. Next, invite each youngster to cut apart the pages and stack them in order with the cover on top. Staple the pages along the left-hand side. When the booklets are finished, invite youngsters to take them home to share with their families!

_____ naps. 1

A _____

_____ naps. 3

A _____

Who Naps?

by _____

_____ naps. 2

A _____

O Is for Officer!

Officer Buckle and Gloria
Written and Illustrated by Peggy Rathmann

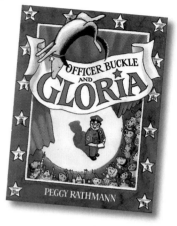

Whenever Officer Buckle delivers his safety tips to Napville School, his assemblies are met with snores—that is until his new police dog, Gloria, comes with him! Unbeknownst to Officer Buckle, Gloria is providing amusing demonstrations of each safety tip he reads. Officer Buckle is upset when he finds out he's being upstaged by a pooch, until he realizes that he and Gloria make the perfect team!

Officer Says...
Using prior knowledge

What safety tips would an officer recommend? Little ones will let you know with this prereading activity! Program a sentence strip with the phrase "An officer would say" and then place it in a pocket chart. Also program separate sentence strips with different safe and unsafe tips (see the suggestions provided). To begin, choose a tip and read it aloud. If the children decide the tip is one a police officer would say, have a youngster place the sentence strip in the pocket chart. If not, have her place the sentence strip in a separate pile. Continue in the same way for each safety tip. When you've finished, read aloud the completed chart. Next, explain to youngsters that the book you're about to read is about a police officer who loves to read safety tips to youngsters—if only he could get them to listen! Then have students settle in for this four-star read-aloud!

Safe and Unsafe Tips:
Look both ways before crossing the street.
Do not play with matches.
Play in parking lots.
Stand on a swivel chair.
Hold on to handrails when using the stairs.
Always wear a helmet when you ride a bike.
Run with scissors in your hand.
Keep your shoelaces tied.

An officer would say

Look both ways before crossing the street.

Do not play with matches.

Hold on to handrails when using the stairs.

Always wear a helmet when you ride a bike.

Keep your shoelaces tied.

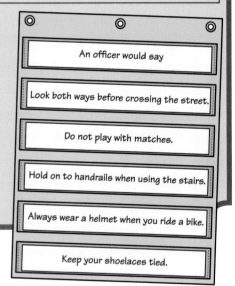

Dear Officer Buckle,
My favorite part of the story is when you and Gloria tell the kids not to sit on a tac.

Dear Officer Buckle
Recalling story details

A young girl from Napville School writes to Officer Buckle on star-shaped paper to thank him for his safety tips. Your youngsters can write Officer Buckle too—with a slightly different goal in mind! Review the story with your students, taking care to point out the star-shaped letters Officer Buckle receives. Next, give each child a large star cutout labeled with the writing prompt shown. Have students complete the prompt and illustrate their writings. Invite youngsters to share their writings with their classmates. Then display the pictures around a banner similar to the one on the cover of the book.

Star Search

Identifying the letter O

Illuminate the letter O with a search for Officer Buckle's badge! Make a class supply of star cutouts (page 62) to represent officers' badges. Then label each badge with a letter, taking care to label only one with the letter O. To begin, revisit the book and point out the badge Officer Buckle wears to show he is a police officer. Choose a youngster to be Officer Buckle and have the remaining children stand in a circle. Give each child in the circle a badge and have him hold it so the letter is visible. Next, explain that Officer Buckle has lost his badge and needs to find it. He'll know which badge is his because it has the letter O on it for *officer*. Then prompt the child to walk around the inside of the circle and inspect the cutouts to find his badge. When he locates it, choose a new Officer Buckle and redistribute all the badges for another round.

Safety Tips
From the
Kindergarten Officers

Safety Tip # 1

Officer __Kendra__ says __alwas ti yor shos.__

Tips Are the Tops

Completing a writing prompt

With this class-made safety book, youngsters are certain to have a safety record that's in tip-top shape! As a class, review some of the safety tips Officer Buckle recommends. Then give each child a copy of page 63. Encourage her to draw her face on the police officer and color the uniform. Then have her write her name in the appropriate blank and complete the prompt with a desired safety tip, providing help as needed. Next, encourage each youngster to illustrate her tip in the space provided. Collect the papers. Beginning with the number 1, write a safety tip number on each page in the space provided. Sequence the pages. Then bind them together in a class book titled "Safety Tips From the [your grade] Officers."

Star Patterns
Use with "Star Search" on page 61.

Safety Tip # _____

Officer _____

says _____

_____

_____

Note to the teacher: Use with "Tips Are the Tops" on page 61.

P Is for Pumpkin!

Pumpkin Pumpkin
Written and Illustrated by Jeanne Titherington

What happens when a young boy plants a tiny pumpkin seed? It grows throughout the summer into a huge pumpkin that's just right for carving! Soft, detailed colored-pencil drawings complement the simple, flowing text to make a wonderful read-aloud classic.

What's Inside?
Using prior knowledge

Grow youngsters' interest in pumpkins with this guessing game. In advance, put a small pumpkin into an opaque tote bag. Close the bag and put it in your story area. Before reading the story, show youngsters the bag and invite them to guess what's inside. Encourage them to gather clues by asking you yes-or-no questions such as the following: Is it round? Is it heavy? Is it an animal? Is it blue? After several clues have been given, have volunteers try to guess what's inside. When the pumpkin is revealed, show youngsters the book and explain that they're going to learn how pumpkins grow.

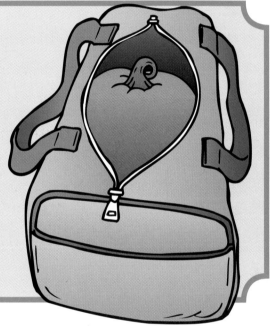

Pass the Pumpkin
Retelling a story

This pleasing pumpkin activity makes retelling the story plenty of fun! Seat students in a circle and hold the pumpkin used in "What's Inside?" on this page. Say, "Jamie plants a pumpkin seed," and pass the pumpkin to the child seated on your right. Have that child tell what happens next and then pass the pumpkin to the next child. Continue passing the pumpkin and retelling story events until each child has had a turn. (You may need to retell the story more than once.) Why, that pumpkin grew and grew and grew!

P

Pick a *P*!
Recognizing letters

Help your students discriminate between *p*, *b*, *d*, and *q* with this challenging sorting activity. To prepare, cut approximately 15 pumpkin seed shapes from tan craft foam. Use a permanent marker to label eight seeds (with the pointed end up) with the letter *p*. Label each remaining seed with *b*, *d*, or *q*. Mix the seeds together and store them in a pumpkin-shaped dish. To complete the activity, a child pours out the seeds and then picks out the *p*'s.

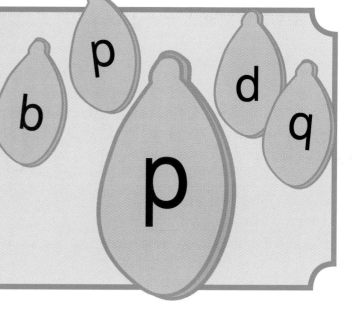

Pumpkin Parts
Using descriptive writing

Use the small pumpkin from "What's Inside?" and "Pass the Pumpkin" on page 64 in a simple exploration activity that's just right for your little learners. Invite youngsters to predict what the inside of the pumpkin will look like; then cut it in half. Divide the class into two groups and give each group one pumpkin half to touch, smell, and examine. Bring students back to the circle, collect the halves, and have students discuss their findings. Label the pumpkin parts by writing each part's name on a separate card, taping a toothpick to the back of the card, and inserting the toothpick into the matching pumpkin part as shown. Ask a few volunteers to think of words to describe each part, such as *orange* and *rough*. Next, give each child a copy of page 67. Invite him to color and label each part. Then have him choose one part to describe. When students are finished, give each child an opportunity to share his description. Yes indeed, the pulp is stringy!

Gooey Pumpkin

Responding to literature through art

This craft is perfect following an opportunity to feel the inside of a real pumpkin. (See "Pumpkin Parts" on page 65.) In advance, cut two identical pumpkin cutouts from 9" x 12" orange construction paper for each child. Also cut identical openings in each set of cutouts, as shown, no larger than six inches in diameter. Give each child a sandwich-size resealable plastic bag. Squirt about one tablespoon of clear or yellow hair gel into each bag. Have each student add a handful of clear cello shred (gift basket filler) to his bag. Next, assist each child in adding ten craft foam pumpkin seeds to his bag. Remove some air before sealing each bag. If desired, reinforce the closures with clear packing tape. Help each youngster tape his bag (at the corners) over the opening in one pumpkin cutout. Then have him put glue on the cutout in the area surrounding the bag and place the remaining cutout atop the glue. For a finishing touch, have the student cut a brown construction paper stem to glue on his pumpkin. Then provide a green construction paper leaf and green curling ribbon for him to glue to his pumpkin. Youngsters will love touching the insides of their gooey pumpkins; and lucky for you, there's no mess!

Pumpkin Parts

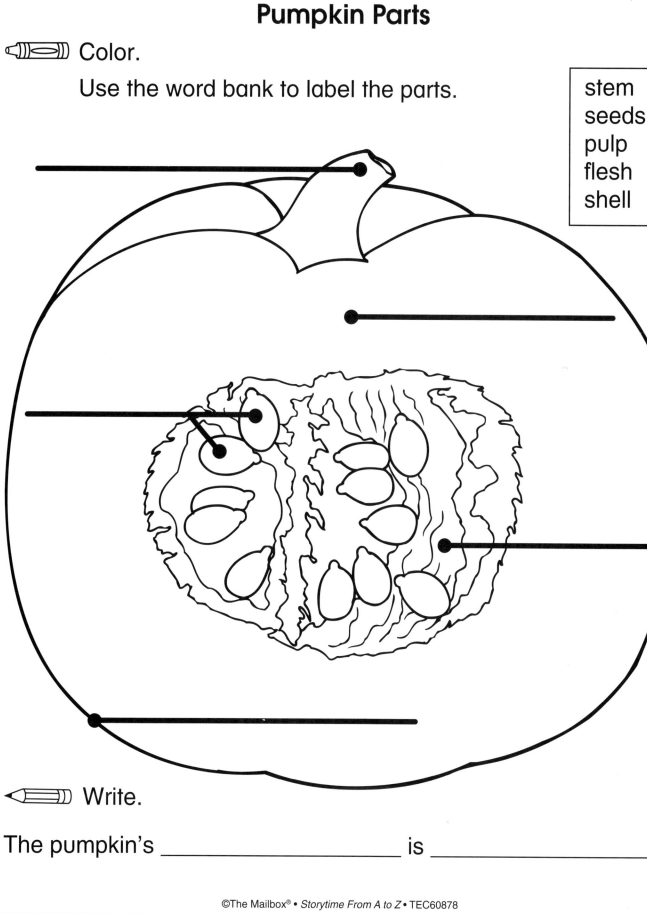

Color.

Use the word bank to label the parts.

stem
seeds
pulp
flesh
shell

Write.

The pumpkin's _____ is _____ .

Note to the teacher: Use with "Pumpkin Parts" on page 65.

Q Is for Quilt!

The Quilt Story
Written by Tony Johnston
Illustrated by Tomie dePaola

A pioneer girl's mother makes a quilt to provide her with warmth and comfort. The little girl cherishes her quilt because it helps her feel at home. Generations later another little girl discovers the quilt in an attic and her mother lovingly mends it. The little girl finds that the quilt comforts her and helps her feel secure. She loves the quilt too. This cozy quilt provides years of security.

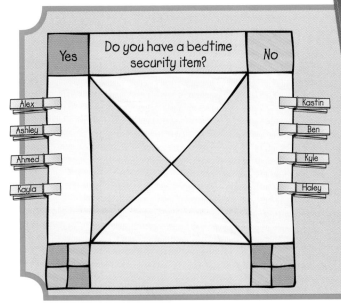

Comforting Quilt
Using prior knowledge

Get comfortable for this graphing activity! In advance, prepare a quilt-shaped graph as shown. Then ask youngsters what they think a quilt is as you show them the cover of the book. Guide them to understand that a quilt is a blanket that provides warmth and often a sense of security, especially at bedtime. Encourage each child to describe a special item that makes her feel secure at bedtime. Then give each child a personalized clothespin. Ask each youngster to answer yes or no to the graph question by attaching her clothespin to the corresponding side of the quilt as shown.

Quick Changes?
Relating the story to personal experience

What a journey that special quilt takes! After reading the story to youngsters, ask them to recall who makes the quilt, whom it belongs to, how it travels, and how it changes over time. Then discuss with youngsters how they have changed since last year. Explain to students that some changes occur quickly, like losing a tooth, and some changes occur slowly, like growing a new tooth. Encourage each child to tell about one thing he can do now that he could not do last year. Next, have him draw and color a picture of himself doing the activity. Then help him write or dictate a sentence describing his illustration.

Q Story
Developing letter-sound awareness

Engage youngsters in creating a quirky *Q* story! Spread a small quilt on a table and then place several objects that begin like *quilt* on it, such as a toy queen, a quartz rock, a toy quail, a quill, and a quart container. Label a card with the name of each object as shown. Show students each object and the corresponding card. Encourage youngsters to repeat the name of each object, emphasizing the beginning sound. Next, ask several youngsters to each choose an object and show it to the class. Then help the group create a story including the chosen objects. Repeat the activity several times with different objects. What a story!

quart

quartz

queen

quail

quill

Name Leah

My Special Quilt

Writing to complete a sentence

My quilt has a...

btrfli

I would use my quilt to...

Keep me wrm

in the wntr

My Special Quilt
Writing to complete a sentence

There's something special about every homemade quilt. Youngsters will enjoy designing their own special quilt blocks for this writing activity. Review the story with youngsters, drawing their attention to the quilt illustrations. Then give each child a copy of page 71 and several colorful paper pattern block shapes. Have her use the shapes to create a unique design on her quilt block. Then help her write or dictate to complete the sentences at the bottom of the page. Encourage each child to share her quilt block and sentences with the class. Then arrange all the blocks in a quilt formation as shown. How cozy!

Quite a Quilt!

Recognizing the letter Q

Quite a nice quilt takes shape with this letter-making project. To prepare, cut a supply of two-inch squares and triangles from wallpaper samples (approximately 12 shapes per child), and cut a nine-inch construction paper square for each child. Program each construction paper square with an uppercase Q. After revisiting the quilt illustration in the story, review the letter Q with youngsters. Then give each child a programmed square and ask him to choose either squares or triangles for his quilt block. Help each child position his shapes on top of his letter Q and then glue each one in place as shown. Later, display all the squares in a quilt formation titled "Quite a Quilt!"

Quite a Quilt!

My Special Quilt

My quilt has a…

_____

I would use my quilt to…

_____

_____

Note to the teacher: Use with "My Special Quilt" on page 69.

71

R Is for Rabbit!

Rabbits and Raindrops
Written and Illustrated by Jim Arnosky

It's raining! It's pouring! When a mother rabbit and her five babies venture out from their home under a hedge, it begins to rain. They hop back under the hedge lickety-split, and a variety of insects and animals join them to wait out the storm.

Out of the Rain
Using prior knowledge

You'll receive an outpouring of ideas when you ask little ones how to stay dry during a rainstorm. Draw two large circles on your board. Label one circle "people" and the other circle "animals." Encourage students to suggest ways people might stay dry during a rainstorm as you write their ideas in the corresponding circle. Then repeat the process, asking students how animals might stay dry. Next, explain that the storytime selection for the day is about a family of rabbits who hide under a hedge to get out of the rain. Add the word *hedge* to the circle labeled "animals." Then have students share what they think a hedge might be. After students have an opportunity to share their thoughts, read the story aloud for them to find out!

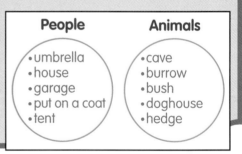

People	Animals
•umbrella	•cave
•house	•burrow
•garage	•bush
•put on a coat	•doghouse
•tent	•hedge

Is it in the story?

Yes	No

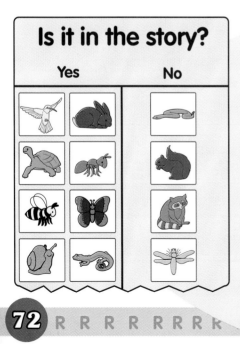

Details, Details
Recalling details from a story

With this second reading of the story, your youngsters are sure to soak up the details! Make a copy of page 75. Color the pictures and laminate them for durability. Then cut the cards apart and place them in a lunch-size paper sack. Title a sheet of chart paper as shown. Then divide it in half and label one side "yes" and the other side "no." Display the paper in your storytime area. As you read the book aloud, have youngsters take note of the small animals and insects in the illustrations. Then have a student choose a card from the sack and announce the name of the animal. Have the class decide whether or not the animal is in the illustrations. Then encourage the youngster to tape the card under the appropriate heading. When all the cards are taped to the chart, revisit the book to check the answers.

Hop! Hop! Hop!
Identifying beginning sounds

Keep little ones hopping with a game that focuses on letter sounds! Gather or make a class supply of picture cards, making sure that several picture things whose names begin with the /r/ sound. Choose a student to be a rabbit (if desired, invite her to don a rabbit headband). Then give each of the remaining students a card, and have the students stand in a circle to represent flowers. Invite the rabbit to hop around the inside of the circle and stand in front of a flower. Encourage the flower to say the name of the picture on his card. Have the rabbit repeat the name and identify whether the word begins with the /r/ sound. Encourage them to trade places. Then invite the new rabbit to go hopping through the flowers.

Rain begins with /r/!

rain | drop

Watching the Raindrops
Combining segments to make a word

No umbrella is needed for this gentle downpour of compound words! Make several large blue construction paper raindrops. Cut each raindrop in half vertically. Then label each set of corresponding halves with a divided compound word as shown, including some from the story. Laminate the raindrops for durability. Present each half of a raindrop and say the words separately. Then, as you prompt students to say the compound word, hold the halves side by side to complete the raindrop. Continue in the same manner with each remaining raindrop. To provide youngsters with more compound word practice, mix up the raindrops and place them at a center.

Drip, Drip, Raindrop

Reinforcing literature through art

Drip, drip, drop! This colorful raindrop display will brighten up any rainy day! To prepare, trace a large raindrop pattern onto a sheet of aluminum foil for each child as shown. Prepare several cups of paint in different shades of blue. Mix a teaspoon of liquid dish soap into each. Tape each prepared foil sheet onto a flat workspace. Invite several youngsters to the paint center. Next, model for youngsters how to dip a cotton swab into one color of paint and then press dots onto the raindrop shape. Then encourage each child to cover his raindrop in dots. After the paint has dried, help him cut out the shape and then glue it onto a slightly larger blue construction paper raindrop shape as shown. Display the completed raindrops on a board embellished with a construction paper hedge. Add paper bunnies, butterflies, and other critters from the story as desired.

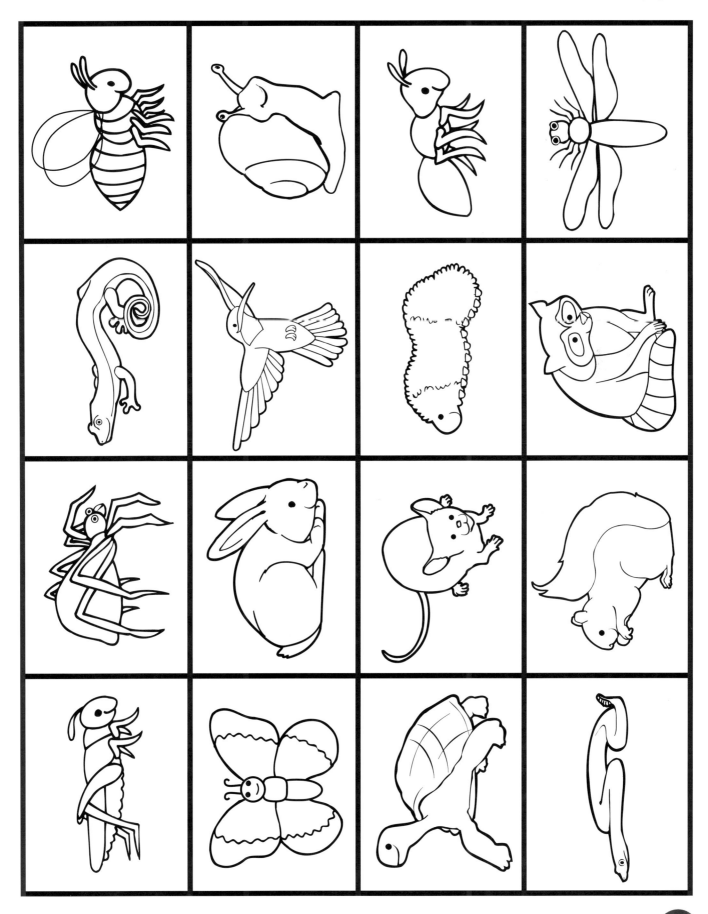

S Is for Sandwich!

The Giant Jam Sandwich

Verses by Janet Burroway
Story and Illustrations by John Vernon Lord

Angry wasps are causing quite a buzz in the town of Itching Down! When the townspeople hold a meeting to decide what to do about the wasps, Bap the Baker proposes that they trap the wasps in a giant jam sandwich. Little ones will be enthralled as they watch the townspeople put this ambitious plan into action to rid the town of the irritating insects!

Recipe for a Sandwich
Building on prior knowledge

Is there a recipe to follow to make a jam sandwich? There will be after your little ones get some firsthand experience making one! Cut a supply of bread slices into quarters. Then give each child a small amount of strawberry jam, a plastic knife, and two prepared pieces of bread. Encourage each youngster to use the supplies to make a small jam sandwich. Then invite him to eat his sandwich. When the children are finished, gather them in your storytime area. Invite them to explain how they made the sandwiches while you write their words on a sheet of chart paper. Next, explain that the book you're about to read is about a group of people who make a jam sandwich using a similar method—only on a much larger scale! Then have youngsters listen to this fun read-aloud.

Put some jam on your knife.
Spread it across the slice of bread.
Lick your fingers.
Put the other slice of bread of top.
Eat your sandwich.
Don't forget to throw away your napkin.

Sandwich Sizes
Identifying words with similar meanings

This writing center display is sure to be hugely popular with your youngsters! Draw a large sandwich on a length of bulletin board paper and post the paper in your story-time area. After a second reading of the story, ask youngsters why the word *giant* is used to describe the sandwich. Have students share their ideas. Then prompt them to think of other words that have meanings similar to the word *giant*. Write each word near the picture of the large sandwich. To extend the idea, draw a picture of a small sandwich near the large one. Ask youngsters to think of words that have meanings similar to the word *small* as you write each one near the small sandwich. Finally, display the paper in your writing center for youngsters to use as inspiration for their own stories!

huge   large   little   small   tiny   gigantic   big   teeny   dinky   jumbo

Capturing the Letter S
Identifying the beginning sound /s/

If a strawberry sandwich is useful for catching wasps, it's sure to be a handy tool for capturing words that begin with the sound of the letter *S*! Enlarge a copy of the picture cards on page 78. Then color the cards and cut them out. Cut two large bread slices from brown bulletin board paper. Also cut a shape from red bulletin board paper to resemble a splotch of jam. Next, place a prepared bread slice in your storytime area and place the jam splotch on top of it. Gather students around the paper. Present one of the picture cards, have students name the picture, and then ask them to identify whether the name begins with the sound of the letter *S*. If it does, invite a child to place it on the jam. If it doesn't, have him place it in a separate pile. Continue in the same way for each picture. Then have youngsters help you lower the remaining slice of bread onto the picture cards to complete the sandwich. For further practice with the sound of the letter *S*, have youngsters complete a copy of page 79. How satisfying!

Favorite Fillings
Writing to complete a sentence

Jam may not be the sandwich filling of choice for your little ones, so have students express their sandwich preferences with this fun booklet! Give each child a bread slice cutout and encourage her to glue cut-paper decorations to it so that it resembles her favorite sandwich filling. Give each youngster a second bread cutout labeled with the prompt "The Giant _____ Sandwich." Have her write (or dictate as you write) her sandwich filling choice in the space provided. Then stack the slices with the prompt on top and staple them together. Display the booklets on a bulletin board titled "Super Sandwiches!"

Picture Cards

Use with "Capturing the Letter *S*" on page 77.

Name _____

A Supersize Sandwich

Glue pictures whose names begin like 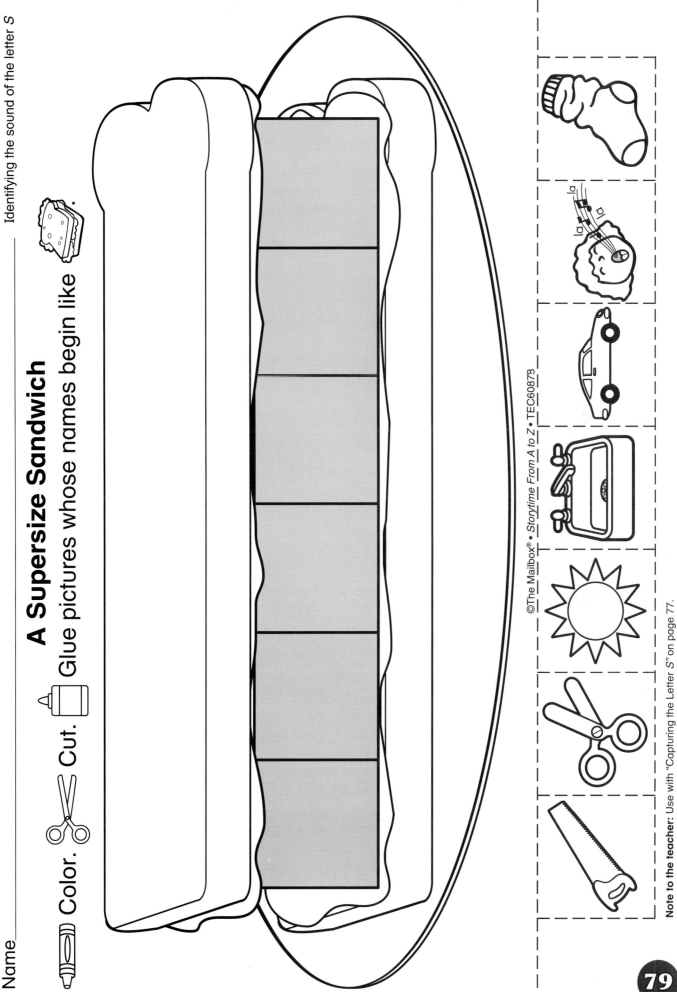.

Color. Cut.

©The Mailbox® • *Storytime From A to Z* • TEC60873

Note to the teacher: Use with "Capturing the Letter *S*" on page 77.

79

T Is for Ten!

Ten Apples Up on Top!
Written by Theo LeSieg
Illustrated by Roy McKie

A lion, a dog, and a tiger have a balancing competition that leads to ten apples on top of each one's head. Their rollicking adventure becomes even more challenging when a bear and some birds try to make the apples on top drop!

Top Ten
Predicting

This "a-peel-ing" graph activity is a real balancing act! Show youngsters the book cover and ask them to describe the action. Next, read the title to students and encourage them to name the words that begin with the /t/ sound. Then show your group a basket of ten apples and a *T*-shaped paper graph programmed as shown. Ask each child to predict whether he could balance ten apples on top of a table. Give each youngster an apple-shaped cutout; then have him answer the question by placing his apple on the corresponding side of the graph. Help students count the results. Then invite one child at a time to test his prediction by trying to balance several apples in a stack.

YES I can balance 10 apples! NO

Orderly Animals
Recalling story details

Who's the first character to put an apple on top? Practice ordinal positions as youngsters sequence the story characters with this small-group activity. In advance, make a copy of the the animal cards on page 82. Color and cut out the cards. If desired, laminate the cards for durability. Next, read the story to students. Review the illustrations and help youngsters count the number of apples each different character balances on his head. Show youngsters the prepared animal cards. Then ask youngsters which of the animals first balances an apple. Have the child who answers correctly place the corresponding card first in a row. Continue with similar questions about the remaining animals. When all the picture cards are sequenced, enlist students' help to review ordinal positions as you point to each animal.

"T-riffic" Tiger!
Identifying the beginning /t/ sound

Grab a tiger by the tail to help reinforce the /t/ sound! To prepare, make a large letter *T* cutout and a copy of page 83 for each child. Use a tiger puppet or a stuffed tiger to introduce the letter *T* and its sound, as in the word *tiger*, to youngsters. Acting as the tiger's voice, ask students to list words that begin with the /t/ sound. Next, give each child a copy of page 83 and a *T* cutout. Still pretending to speak for the tiger, name each picture aloud. Then ask each child to color and cut out the pictures. Have each child name each picture, sorting those whose names begin with the /t/ sound onto his letter *T*. Ask him to glue each *T* picture in place and then count to insure he has ten pictures. Have the tiger give encouragement as it checks each child's work. Grrreat!

TEN!

10 Balancing Act
Writing to complete a sentence

Can you balance ten on top? Youngsters will enjoy experimenting with balance as they complete this whimsical writing activity. For each child, program a 12" x 18" sheet of paper with the partial sentence shown. Then review the sections of the story where the animals are balancing ten apples on top of their heads. Ask youngsters to name different things that they would like to balance on top of their heads. Record students' answers on a chart. Next, give each child a programmed sheet and help her write or dictate to finish the sentence, referring to the chart if needed. Then have her draw a picture of her head with the ten objects on top. Encourage each child to share her sentence and illustration with the class. Be sure to allow time for giggles!

I can balance 10 _flowers_.
Alyson

Animal Cards

Use with "Orderly Animals" on page 80.

U Is for Underwear!

Underwear!
Written by Mary Elise Monsell

Zachary Zebra and Orfo Orangutan have a great collection of underwear that their friend Bismark the grumpy buffalo doesn't appreciate. Zachary, Orfo, and the other grassland animals want to help Bismark. So the animals devise an underwear plan to get Bismark to laugh out loud.

A Flair for Underwear
Distinguishing between reality and fantasy

Who wears underwear? What a silly question; everyone does! That may be your youngsters' answer until they complete this prereading activity. Show youngsters a stuffed animal dressed in a pair of children's underwear and have them tell you about the animal's clothing. Is it appropriate? Next, show students the book cover. Ask youngsters whether real animals wear underwear and encourage them to tell why or why not. Then set the tone for the story by putting the underwear on the stuffed animal's head. After the giggles subside, read the story to your little ones.

Grumpy to Giddy
Recalling story details

Don't laugh! Play this action game to change grumpy attitudes to giddy fun. After reading the story to youngsters, ask them to recall how Bismark Buffalo shows everyone he is grumpy. Next, ask them to tell what the other animals do to make Bismark laugh. Does underwear have anything to do with it? At circle time, select one child to sit in the center of the group. Ask her to pretend to be grumpy Bismark and have her wear a paper buffalo-horn headband as shown. Invite one child at a time to do a silly action to try to make Bismark laugh. When Bismark laughs, have her pass the headband to the next grumpy buffalo. Dare him not to laugh!

My Underwear!
Recognizing the short U sound

Singing about underwear may cause an uproar of laughter during this fun phonics activity. To prepare, program a copy of page 87 with an uppercase and a lowercase *U*; then make a class supply. Give each child a copy and ask him to use his finger to trace the letters. Next, sing the song for youngsters. Then encourage each child to trace the letters as he sings the short *U* sound in the song.

(sung to the tune of "Skip to My Lou")

/u/, /u/, underwear,
/u/, /u/, underwear,
/u/, /u/, underwear—
I love to wear my underwear!
/u/, /u/, under my pants,
/u/, /u/, under my shorts,
/u/, /u/, under my jammies—
I love to wear my underwear!

Designer Undies
Writing to complete a sentence

Design the ultimate pair of underwear! Encourage youngsters' creativity with this class book-making project. Give each child a copy of the underwear pattern on page 87. Help her write or dictate to complete the sentence "I like underwear with…" Have her illustrate her underwear to match her sentence. Then help her cut out the underwear shape. Collect the completed underwear shapes and staple them together with a cover as shown. Read the book to the class and then place it in the book center for all to enjoy.

Designer Undies
by
Mrs. Leonard's class

Undershirts!
Extending the story through art

It's okay to show off these unbelievable undershirts! In advance, collect a new white T-shirt for each child and gather different colors of fabric paint. Review the illustrations in the story with youngsters, noticing Zachary's and Orfo's colorful patterned underwear and plain undershirts. Ask students which underwear pattern they like best: polka-dotted, striped, flowered, or another design? Next, help each child paint a similar pattern on her undershirt. After the shirts dry, hang them on a clothesline at youngsters' eye level. Next, gather your group and observe each undershirt. Then guide them to use the characters from *Underwear!* to create a new story titled *Undershirts!*

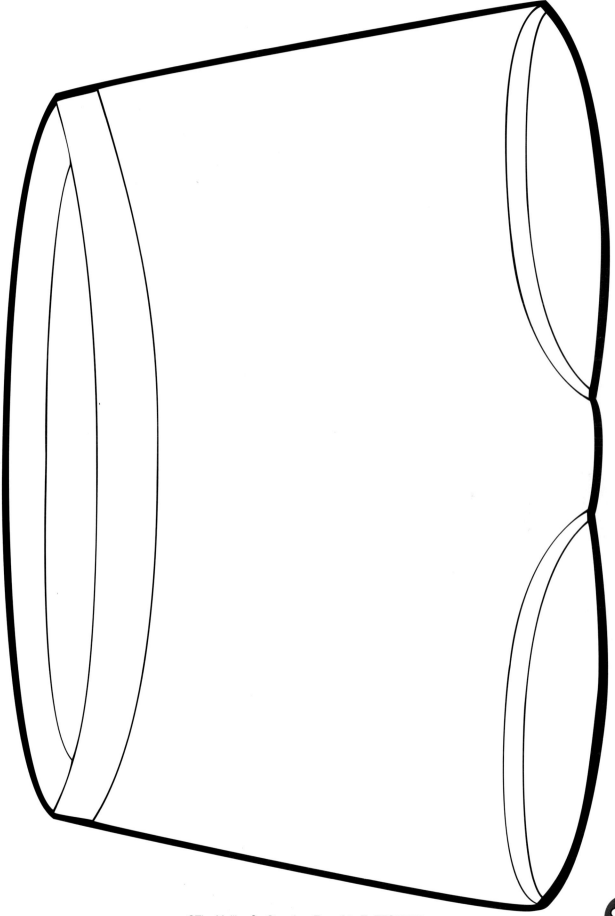

V Is for Vegetable!

Growing Vegetable Soup
Written and Illustrated by Lois Ehlert

A child and her father plant and grow a vegetable garden that provides the ingredients for a pot full of delicious vegetable soup. Each step, from what happens in the garden to putting the veggies in the soup, is described. Yum!

Growing Vegetable Soup

Written and illustrated by Lois Ehlert

Know Your Vegetables
Using prior knowledge

Before reading the story, use this activity to find out what your youngsters know about vegetables. Ahead of time, gather a supply of different types of vegetables, such as those mentioned in the book. Next, show the vegetables one at a time while asking your youngsters to identify them. Explain that vegetables are served in many different kinds of dishes, such as salads, casseroles, and soups. Then introduce the book by discussing the title and cover art.

seed   sprout   plant   vegetable   pot   soup

From Seeds to Soup
Sequencing story events

Sprout little ones' story recall skills with this sequencing activity! In advance, prepare a set of simple sequencing cards as shown. Next, share *Growing Vegetable Soup* with students. Ask youngsters to recall the various steps for growing vegetables and making vegetable soup. Then randomly show each sequencing card, inviting students to share related story events. Have volunteers place the cards in order and explain their reasoning. Finally, revisit the story to check the sequence. Voilà! "Seed-sational" sequencing!

Sounds Like Veggies
Recognizing the /v/ sound

What better time to develop your young-sters' awareness of the /v/ sound than during an investigation of vegetables! Write the word *vegetable* on the board. Emphasize the initial /v/ sound as you guide the class in reading the word aloud a few times. Next, ask students to name other words that begin with the same sound. Write each word on the board and guide the class in reading it aloud. Invite a volunteer to trace with colored chalk each *V*. Conclude the activity by chal-lenging each child to use her knowledge of the /v/ sound to complete a copy of page 90. Hey, that begins like *vegetable!*

Name Samantha

Writing to complete a sentence

My vegetable soup has... broccoli and carrots

Soup's On!
Writing to complete a sentence

Serve up some delicious writing practice! Make a class supply of page 91. Next, prepare four stations in your art area for vegetable printing, featuring a different veggie at each one. (Vegetables that will work well include a zucchini, a potato, a carrot, a stalk of broccoli, or a pepper.) Then write the name of each featured vege-table on a tagboard strip and stamp its print.

Show students a sample of each vegetable and display the strip that shows its name and print. Give each child a copy of the sentence starter. Have her choose two vegetable names and copy them onto her paper to complete the sentence. Provide assistance as necessary. Then have her lightly color soup broth in the bowl. Next, move the tagboard strips to their corresponding stations. Arrange for each child to find the matching vegetable words and print the appropriate veggies in her soup. Be sure to invite each child to share her mouthwatering masterpiece with the class!

Name

The Vegetable View

Color the pictures that begin like 🏺.

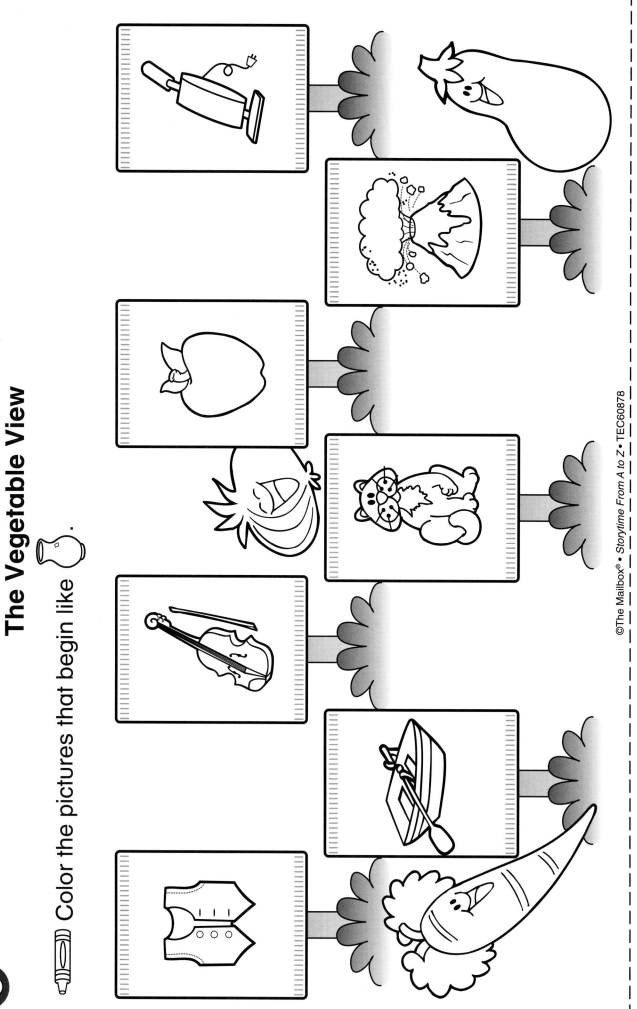

Note to the teacher: Use with "Sounds Like Veggies" on page 89.

Name _____

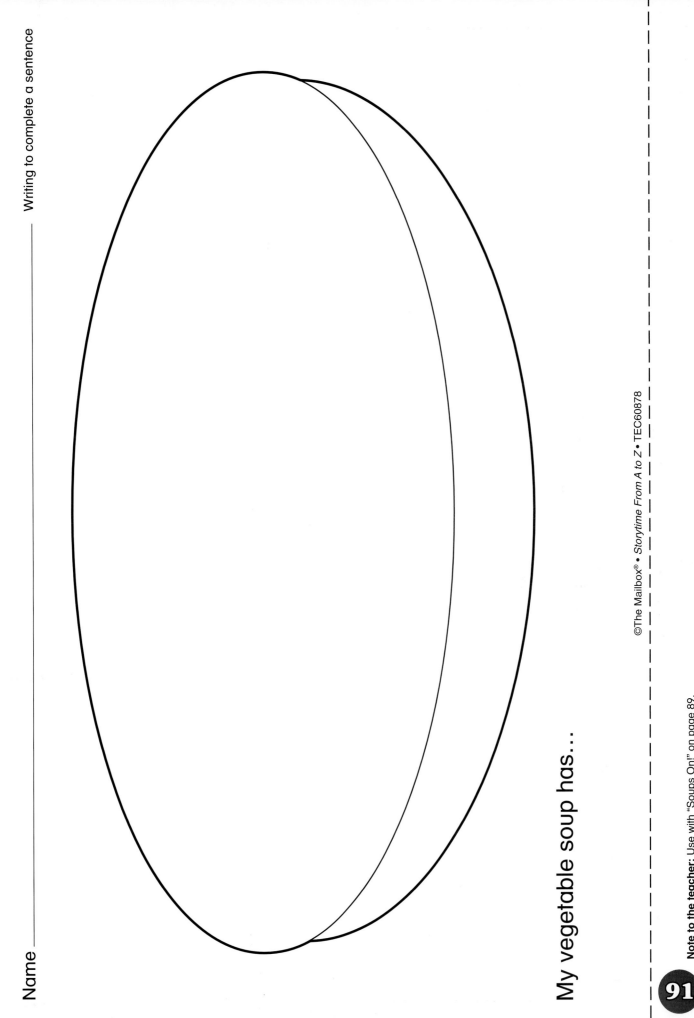

My vegetable soup has...

Note to the teacher: Use with "Soups On!" on page 89.

W Is for Wild!

Where the Wild Things Are
Written and Illustrated by Maurice Sendak

When Max gets into trouble for his wild behavior, he is sent to his room without his supper. That night, his room transforms into a jungle, and he sails to the land where the wild things are. After taking part in a wild rumpus and being named king of the wild things, he finds himself feeling quite lonely. So he decides to sail back to the place where he is loved best of all!

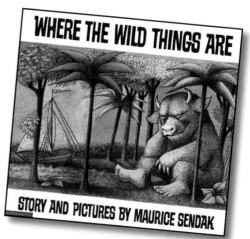

What Is Wild?
Building on prior knowledge

Draw on youngsters' knowledge of the word *wild* to help them visualize what a wild thing might look like! Draw a simple body outline on a sheet of chart paper and then post the paper in your storytime area. Before reading the story, ask students to share what they think *wild* means. After students share several ideas, ask them what a wild thing might look like. As they describe each feature, draw it on the outline. Next, show the book's cover and explain that the story you're about to read is about a little boy who visits a land inhabited by wild things. Then read the story aloud. When the story is finished, ask youngsters if their wild thing is similar in any way to the wild things in the book!

A Toothy Tale
Identifying beginning, middle, and end

These wild things' toothy grins conceal a booklet that shows the sequence of events in the story! Give each child a 6" x 18" piece of white construction paper divided into three equal sections and labeled as shown. Revisit the book with your youngsters and help them identify events that occur in the beginning, middle, and end of the story. Then encourage each youngster to draw a picture to represent each section. Help each student fold her paper into thirds. Then have her glue the resulting booklet to a colorful construction paper oval as shown. Encourage the youngster to transform the project into a wild thing by drawing teeth on the outside of the booklet and adding construction paper features. Finally, post the wild things on a bulletin board. What a monstrously fun display!

| beginning | middle | end |

inside view

Who's a Wild Thing?
Developing phonemic awareness

Giggles abound when little ones identify the names of class-mates with this playful song! Lead youngsters in singing the provided song, replacing the name with a student's name that's been altered to begin with the /w/ sound. At the end of the song, have young-sters guess the child's real name. Wennifer? Why, that's Jennifer! For more practice with the sound of the letter *W*, have each youngster complete a copy of page 95.

Wild Thing Song
(sung to the tune of "London Bridge")

[Wennifer]'s a wild thing,
Wild thing, wild thing.
[Wennifer]'s a wild thing.
Who is [Wennifer]?

Go Away, Max
Completing a writing prompt

Roaring voices, rolling eyes, and gnashing teeth—the wild things try a variety of methods to scare Max. With this writing prompt activity, you can find out what methods your little ones might use if they were wild things! Review the book with your class, taking care to point out actions the wild things use to try to scare Max. Ask youngsters what they might do as wild things to scare Max away. After listening to several ideas, give each child a sheet of white construction paper labeled with the prompt shown. Have him complete the sentence. Then encourage each child to add an illustration to match. Finally, invite each youngster to take his paper home to share with his family.

If I were a wild thing, I would stmp mi fet and yell rele lad.

Wild Thing Footprints
Responding to literature through art

How can a person tell whether there is a wild thing nearby? Why, look for its footprints, of course! Invite youngsters to make this mural covered with wild thing footprints. To begin, tape a length of green bulletin board paper to a table in your art area. Cut different footprint shapes from jumbo sponges as shown. Place each prepared sponge in a shallow container of colorful tempera paint. Then place the containers at the table. To begin, revisit the book and prompt youngsters to notice the wild things' varied feet. Invite a small group of children to the table. Have each child choose a sponge and then use it to make prints on the paper. After each child in your class has had an opportunity to paint, set the project aside to dry. Then display the finished mural in your classroom!

Wonderful Wild Things
Responding to literature through song

Remind youngsters of a wild thing's unique characteristics with this toe-tapping tune! Lead youngsters in singing the song. After several repetitions, have them sing as they dance around during their own wild rumpus!

(sung to the tune of "Take Me Out to the Ballgame")

Wild things have roaring voices.
Wild things have pointy claws.
They gnash their teeth, and they roll their eyes.
I won't kid you—I'm not telling lies.
They are scary, hairy, and furry.
They howl, they growl, and they sing.
Oh, it would be great fun to sail off and be their king!

Name _____

A Wild Thing King

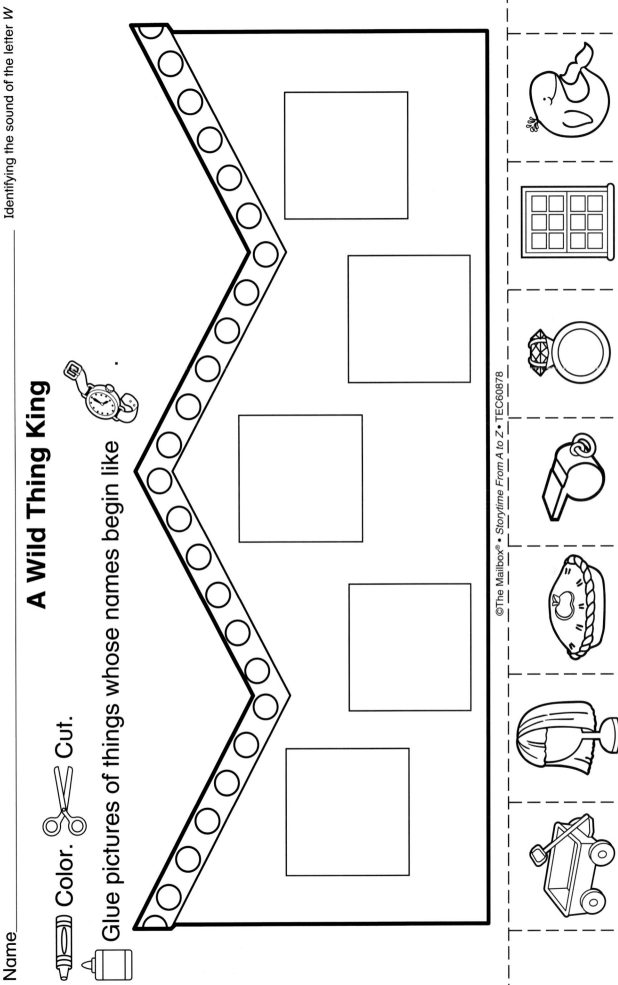

Color. ✂ Cut.

Glue pictures of things whose names begin like ⌚ .

©The Mailbox® • *Storytime From A to Z* • TEC60878

Note to the teacher: Use with "Who's a Wild Thing?" on page 93.

95

X Is for Fox!

Fox in Socks
Written and Illustrated by Dr. Seuss

Where would a fox wear socks in a box with clocks? In Dr Seuss's rhythmic, rhyming world, of course! But be careful reading this tricky fox's word play—after twisting through this tale, your tongue just may be numb.

Thumbs-Up, Thumbs-Down
Recognizing rhyming words

This book is chock-full of rhyming words, so play this game to warm up students for the silly rhymes to come! Gather students and tell them to listen for words that rhyme. Ask them to signal a rhyming pair by holding up their thumbs. If a pair does not rhyme, ask students to point their thumbs down. Then slowly say pairs of rhyming words. Use real and nonsense words to set the tone for the story. After several rounds, challenge youngsters to listen for words that rhyme with *fox* as you read the story. Fox in socks? That's a thumbs-up for sure!

What's That Sound?
Identifying phoneme placement

After hearing the story, students will certainly be familiar with words like *fox* that end with the /ks/ sound. Most likely, your youngsters will have also noticed all the energetic positions the characters take. Combine the two for a phoneme-placement activity that's sure to get the wiggles out! Reread the first page and invite each student to make an X with her body each time she hears the /ks/ at the end of a word. Continue rereading various pages while students listen for ending phonemes. (There are many examples in the first 22 pages.) End the activity by rereading the last page while inviting each child to make her largest X possible. Now that's a fun way to get the wiggles out!

Fox in a Box?

Associating letters with sounds

Provide plenty of practice with the letter *X* and its sound using a box—a favorite of Knox and the fox! In advance, label one side of a small box "Fox" and the opposite side "Knox." Enlarge the picture cards on page 98 if desired; then color and cut them out. During group time, reread the first five pages of the story to remind students of the box that Knox and the fox get into. Then hold up a picture card and ask students to read the word or identify the picture. If the word ends with the letter *X*, put the card in the box. If it does not end with *X*, put the card in a discard pile. After sorting all the cards, remove the ones from the box and review them with students. Then place all the cards and the box in a center for further practice.

This fox wears pink socks and stood in a box eating cake with a rake!

Fox Did What?

Writing rhyming sentences

Have you ever seen a fox wear socks? In a box? With clocks? Probably not, but it's fun to make up silly rhymes starring that rascally fox! Invite youngsters to create their own rhymes and write them on these crafty fox projects. To make a fox, a child glues a red construction paper copy of the fox head pattern (page 99) onto a 4½" by 12" red paper rectangle. She adds construction paper legs and a tail and then uses a marker to add desired details. Next, she cuts four socks from wallpaper samples or scrap paper and glues them to her fox. While the glue dries, she brainstorms a silly rhyme about her fox. Help her write her rhyme on her fox's body. Now where did that fox in pink socks go?

Picture Cards
Use with "Fox in a Box?" on page 97.

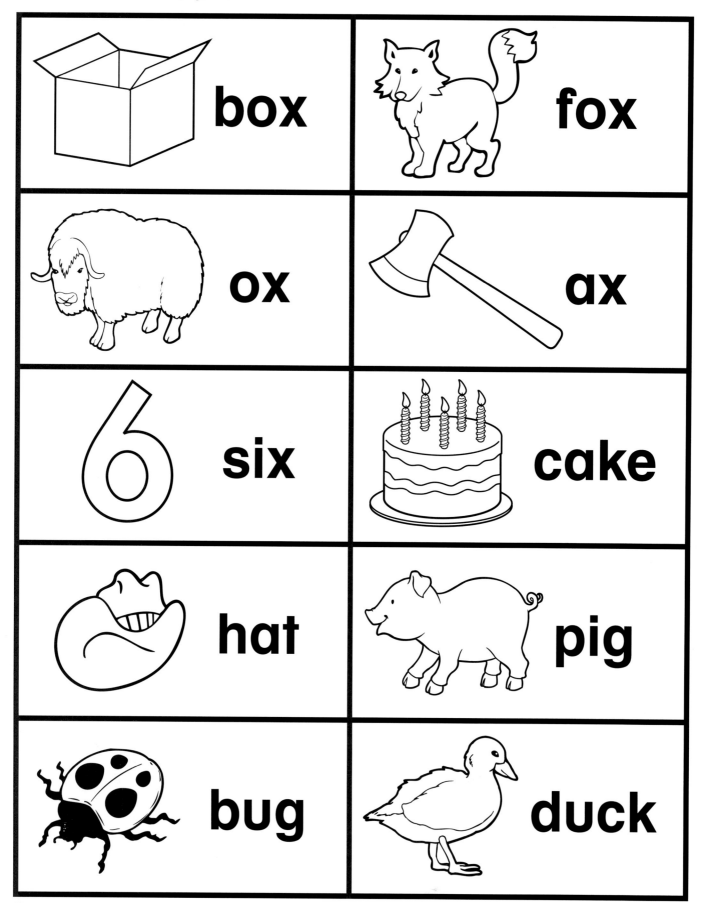

box

fox

ox

ax

six

cake

hat

pig

bug

duck

Y Is for Yellow!

Little Blue and Little Yellow
Written and Illustrated by Leo Lionni

Little blue and little yellow are best friends
who share many colorful adventures. One day,
they learn how well their friendship blends when
they give each other a great big hug.

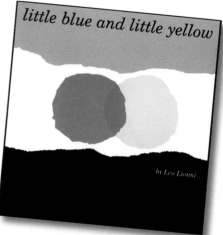

little blue and little yellow

by Leo Lionni

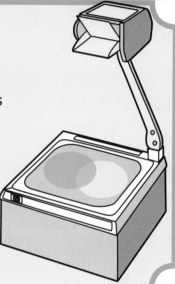

Friends That Blend
Predicting

A little blue and a little yellow are a great mix! Introduce youngsters to
the story with this colorful observation. In advance, set up an overhead
projector and cut out a yellow and a blue cellophane circle. Place the circles
on the overhead and ask youngsters to identify each color. Introduce little
blue and little yellow to students and explain that they are best friends.
Invite youngsters to name some things they like to do with their friends.
Then tell your group that little blue and little yellow like to give each other
hugs to show their friendship. But when these two friends hug, something
special happens. Ask youngsters to predict what they think will happen
when little blue and little yellow hug. Invite a student to move the circles
together until they overlap, revealing the two colors blending into green.
Then read this colorful friendship story to your group.

Lighten Up
Recalling story events

Illuminate youngsters' recall skills with this fun color-mixing activity. To
prepare, gather several flashlights and cut out several different-colored
cellophane circles, including yellow and blue. Attach each circle to a
different flashlight with tape as shown (add several layers of cellophane for
a darker color). After reading the story to youngsters, ask them to tell what
little blue and little yellow do with their friends (*play hide-and-seek, run,
jump, sit still at school, hug*). Then give each of several students a flashlight
and turn off the classroom lights. Ask students to shine the flashlights on a
wall or the ceiling as the class names each color. Help students manipulate
the colored lights to imitate the book's illustrations of the friends' activities,
including hugs!

Yummy Yogurt
Building letter-sound awareness

Would little yellow think yogurt is yummy? Reinforce phonemic-awareness skills with this tasty graphing activity. To prepare, make a yellow construction paper copy of a yogurt cup pattern on page 102 for each child and program a two column graph as shown. Then stir a few drops of yellow food coloring into lemon yogurt to make enough for your class. Give each child a serving of yellow yogurt to taste. Ask students whether the yellow yogurt is yummy. Then read aloud the graph text, emphasizing the /y/ sound at the beginning of the words. Have each child personalize a yogurt cup pattern. Then help her tape her pattern to the corresponding column on the graph. Is yellow yogurt yummy? Yes!

Is Yellow Yogurt Yummy?

Yes	No

Little Yellow's Favorite Game
Beginning /y/ sound

Everyone enjoys a good game of hide-and-seek! But little yellow especially loves to hide behind the beginning /y/ sound pictures in this version of the game. Color and cut apart an enlarged copy of the picture cards on page 103. Place the cards in a pocket chart. Next, hide a yellow construction paper smiley face behind each picture that begins with the /y/sound. Gather your group and discuss the beginning /y/ sound students hear in *yellow*. Tell youngsters that little yellow wants to play hide-and-seek with them and he is hiding behind some of the picture cards. Explain to students that little yellow only hides behind pictures that begin with the /y/ sound. Then invite one child at a time to name a picture and then tell whether it begins with the /y/ sound or not. Help him check his answer by seeking little yellow behind the card. Ready or not, here we come!

In the Mix
Fine-motor skills

When little blue and little yellow mix, does green always appear? Invite your little ones to explore the answer to that question with this hands-on activity. Tell youngsters that little blue and little yellow have come to visit. Then give each child a small ball of yellow play dough and a small ball of blue play dough. Have each child push the two balls together to make them "hug" as in the story. Guide her to observe any changes in the the two colors of play dough. Then ask each child to squeeze and knead the two colors together to make one ball. Lead students to discover that blue and yellow do indeed mix into green.

Yogurt Cup Pattern
Use with "Yummy Yogurt" on page 101.

Name_____

Yummy
YOGURT

Z Is for Zoo!

Zoo-Looking
by Mem Fox
Illustrated by Candace Whitman

When Flora visits the zoo, she gazes at a variety of exciting, interesting, and unique animals. And to Flora's pleasure, some of the animals gaze back at her! But the most memorable part of her trip is when she looks at her father, and he returns her gaze with a smile!

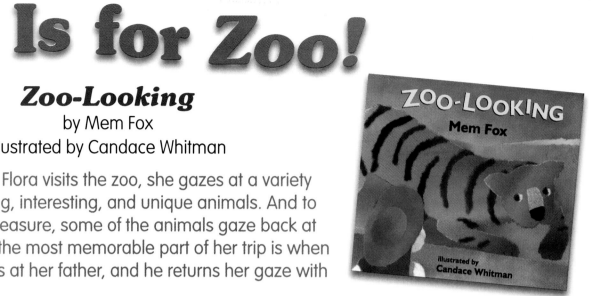

Animals, Animals, Everywhere!
Using prior knowledge

Zebras, monkeys, tigers—a zoo is filled with so many interesting creatures! Build on youngsters' prior knowledge of zoo animals with this roaringly fun prereading activity. Ask students to name several animals that might live in a zoo. Write each child's response on a sheet of chart paper. Then explain that the book you're about to read is about a girl who visits a zoo and sees many different animals. Have youngsters settle in for a reading of the story. After the read-aloud, have youngsters recall the animals in the story and then see whether they are listed on the chart paper. If an animal's name isn't shown, add it to the list!

lion
tiger
bear
monkey
panda
hippo
snake

Zoo Clues
Sequencing story events

Your little zoologists are sure to enjoy answering zoo riddles to re-create the order of events in the story! Label a sheet of chart paper with the sentences shown, leaving out the animals' names and extending the chart to show a space for each animal in the story. Post the chart paper in your circle-time area. To begin, open the book to the page that shows the first zoo animal Flora sees—a giraffe. Give students hints to the animal's identity, such as "This zoo animal is yellow with brown spots and is very tall." When students guess the animal's name, show them the picture and then write the name in the first space on the chart paper. Continue in the same fashion, writing each new animal name in the next available space. When students understand the activity, call on different children to help supply the hints for each remaining animal. Then encourage students to help you read the completed chart.

One day Flora went to the zoo.
She saw a <u>giraffe.</u>
She saw a <u>panther.</u>
She saw a <u>tiger.</u>
She saw a <u>snake.</u>
She saw a <u>penguin.</u>
She saw a <u>monkey.</u>

A Zoo Full of Zs
Substituting beginning sounds

Giggles abound when youngsters change each zoo animal's name so that it begins with the letter *Z*! Divide a length of white bulletin board paper into 14 squares. Then display the paper in your circle-time area. To begin, review the animals in the story with your youngsters. Then give each child a sheet of 9" x 12" white construction paper and have her draw her favorite story animal. Have her cut her picture out. Help youngsters sort the animals on the prepared paper by taping them in place. (Plan to prepare a cutout for any animal not represented.)

Next, explain that the zoo has a rule that all animals living there must have names that begin with the /z/ sound. After confirming that most of the animals' names don't begin with the /z/ sound, encourage youngsters to alter each name so it conforms to the zoo's rule. For example, prompt students to replace the /t/ sound in *tiger* with the /z/ sound to make the new name *ziger*. Then write the animal's new name at the bottom of the corresponding square. For more practice with the letter *Z*, have each youngster complete a copy of page 107!

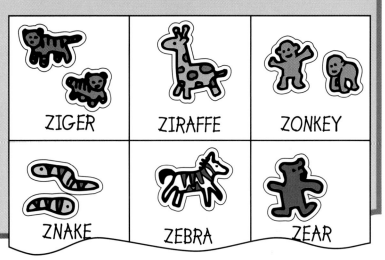

ZIGER ZIRAFFE ZONKEY

ZNAKE ZEBRA ZEAR

Watchful Critters
Completing a writing prompt

When youngsters create a page for this class zoo book, they can look at an animal of their choosing—and it can "look" right back! Make a copy of the prompt shown for each child, leaving off the words in the blanks. Have her write her name in the first space and the name of a chosen zoo animal in the remaining space. Then have her glue the prompt to the bottom of a sheet of 12" x 18" white construction paper. Above the prompt, invite each child to make a collage-style zoo animal by cutting and then gluing a variety of papers, such as tissue paper, construction paper scraps, and wallpaper samples. When the pages are dry, bind them together in a book titled "[Your Name]'s Class Goes to the Zoo!"

Ms. M's Class Goes to the Zoo!

Sammy looked at a _liun_, and it looked back!

Zany Zoo
Responding to literature through art

Everyone will be captivated by this display of zany zoo animals! Before you begin, invite students to offer their definitions for the word *zany*. Then share that it describes someone or something that looks or acts very silly and might make others laugh. Prepare a 6" x 9" sheet of colorful tagboard for each child. Also gather old, assorted zoo animal pictures such as those from magazines. To make a zany animal, encourage each child to cut out various animal parts and glue them onto her tagboard in any silly combination. For added learning, ask each child to name her animal. Write the name on an adhesive address label and attach it to the tagboard backing. Display the cages of zany animals in a hallway display titled "Our Zany Zoo!" Expect lots of onlookers!

Giraf-a-lion

A Zoo Sing-Along
Responding to a story through song

This zippy song will remind your little ones of the fascinating critters that live in a zoo!

(sung to the tune of "Kookaburra")

Zoos are full of critters both large and small,
Some that fly and slither, and some that crawl.
They roar and growl,
Squeak, hiss, and howl.
Zoos are fun for all!

Welcome to
Our Zoo!

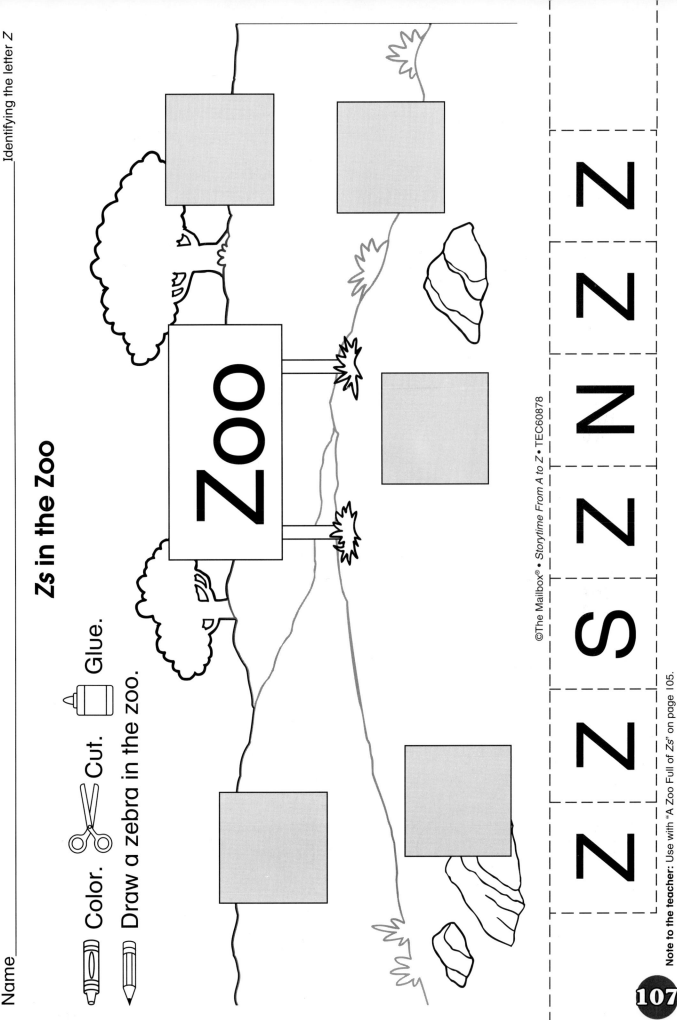

Name

Zs in the Zoo

Color.

Cut.

Glue.

Draw a zebra in the zoo.

ZOO

Z Z Z

Z N Z

Z S Z

Note to the teacher: Use with "A Zoo Full of *Zs*" on page 105.

Book Notes

How to Use the Book Notes

After sharing each picture book and its accompanying activities, make one or more copies of the following book notes. Then complete the following as desired.

- Send a book note home in a bag with its corresponding book.
- Have students use story journals to keep track of featured books. To make a story journal for each child, bind drawing paper between two sheets of construction paper. Have each child personalize his cover as desired. Then, as you give students each book note, instruct each child to glue the note to a page in his journal. If desired, have students take their journals home and list words beginning with the book's featured letter on the same page.
- Create a paper headband for each child and glue a book note to the front of it.
- Have each student tape a book note to her shirt and wear it as a badge.

Book Notes

Use with the directions above.

We read ***There's an Alligator Under My Bed*** by Mercer Mayer.

Let's name words that begin like *alligator!*

©The Mailbox® • *Storytime From A to Z* • TEC60878

We listened to ***Barnyard Banter*** by Denise Fleming.

Help me look for words that begin with the letter *B.*

©The Mailbox® • *Storytime From A to Z* • TEC60878

We read **The Very Hungry Caterpillar** by Eric Carle and learned about the letter *C*.

©The Mailbox® • *Storytime From A to Z* • TEC60878

We read **Make Way for Ducklings** by Robert McCloskey.

Let's name words that begin like *duck*.

©The Mailbox® • *Storytime From A to Z* • TEC60878

We heard **Green Eggs and Ham** by Dr. Seuss.

Help me name words that begin like *egg*.

©The Mailbox® • *Storytime From A to Z* • TEC60878

Our story today was **Fish Eyes: A Book You Can Count On** by Lois Ehlert.

Let's search for words that begin with *F*.

©The Mailbox® • *Storytime From A to Z* • TEC60878

We learned about the letter *G* as we read **Good Night, Gorilla** by Peggy Rathmann. Ask me about it!

©The Mailbox® • *Storytime From A to Z* • TEC60878

We read **A House for Hermit Crab** by Eric Carle.

Help me look around our house for things that start with *H*.

©The Mailbox® • *Storytime From A to Z* • TEC60878

Book Notes

Use with the directions on page 108.

We read **The Itsy Bitsy Spider** by Iza Trapani and learned about itsy-bitsy things.

Help me think of words that begin like *itsy-bitsy.*

©The Mailbox® • *Storytime From A to Z* • TEC60878

We learned about the letter *J* as we read **Jamberry** by Bruce Degen.

Ask me about it!

©The Mailbox® • *Storytime From A to Z* • TEC60878

We read **Miss Bindergarten Gets Ready for Kindergarten** by Joseph Slate.

Help me look around our house for things that start with *K* like *kindergarten.*

©The Mailbox® • *Storytime From A to Z* • TEC60878

We read **Lunch** by Denise Fleming and learned about the letter *L.*

©The Mailbox® • *Storytime From A to Z* • TEC60878

We read **Mud** by Mary Lyn Ray.

Let's name words that begin like *mud.*

©The Mailbox® • *Storytime From A to Z* • TEC60878

We heard **The Napping House** by Audrey Wood.

Help me search for words that begin with the letter *N.*

©The Mailbox® • *Storytime From A to Z* • TEC60878

We read **Officer Buckle and Gloria** by Peggy Rathmann.

Let's name words that begin like *officer.*

©The Mailbox® • *Storytime From A to Z* • TEC60878

We read **Pumpkin Pumpkin** by Jeanne Titherington.

Help me think of words that begin like *pumpkin.*

©The Mailbox® • *Storytime From A to Z* • TEC60878

We heard **The Quilt Story** by Tony Johnston.

Help me search for words that begin with the letter *Q.*

©The Mailbox® • *Storytime From A to Z* • TEC60878

We learned about the letter *R* as we read **Rabbits and Raindrops** by Jim Arnosky.

Ask me about it!

©The Mailbox® • *Storytime From A to Z* • TEC60878

We read **The Giant Jam Sandwich** by John Vernon Lord and Janet Burroway.

Help me look around our house for things that start with *S* like *sandwich.*

©The Mailbox® • *Storytime From A to Z* • TEC60878

We read **Ten Apples Up on Top!** by Dr. Seuss and learned about the letter *T.*

Help me find ten things around our house that start with *T.*

©The Mailbox® • *Storytime From A to Z* • TEC60878

Book Notes

Use with the directions on page 108.

We read **Underwear!** by Mary Elise Monsell.

Help me name things that start with *U* like *underwear.*

©The Mailbox® • *Storytime From A to Z* • TEC60878

We read **Growing Vegetable Soup** by Lois Ehlert and learned about the letter *V.*

Let's name words that start with *V.*

©The Mailbox® • *Storytime From A to Z* • TEC60878

We read **Where the Wild Things Are** by Maurice Sendak.

Let's name words that begin with the letter *W.*

©The Mailbox® • *Storytime From A to Z* • TEC60878

We read **Fox in Socks** by Dr. Seuss and learned about the letter *X.*

Help me think of words that begin or end with *X.*

©The Mailbox® • *Storytime From A to Z* • TEC60878

We learned about the letter *Y* as we read **Little Blue and Little Yellow** by Leo Lionni.

Ask me about it!

©The Mailbox® • *Storytime From A to Z* • TEC60878

We heard **Zoo-Looking** by Mem Fox and learned about the letter *Z.*

Help me think of words that begin with this letter.

©The Mailbox® • *Storytime From A to Z* • TEC60878